Madrid

DIRECTIONS

CALLE DE LAS HUERTAS

WRITTEN AND RESEARCHED BY

Simon Baskett

Contents

Introduction to

Madrid

The sunniest, highest and leafiest capital city in Europe, Madrid has a lot to take pride in. Indeed, its inhabitants, the Madrileños, are so proud of their city that they modestly declare "desde Madrid al Cielo": that from Madrid there is only one destination left – Heaven. While their claim might be debatable, this compact, lively and fascinating city certainly has bags of appeal and its range of attractions is fast making it a deservedly popular short-break destination.

► The bear and strawberry tree, Madrid's emblem

What had previously been a Moorish stronghold and then a small Christian garrison town became Spain's capital in 1561 thanks to the whim of one man, Felipe II. The site possessed few natural advantages – a fierce climate, no harbour and a poor excuse for a river – but it lay exactly in the centre of Spain, and Felipe based the formerly itinerant court here to avoid giving too much power to any one region. Following an initial golden age when

When to visit

Traditionally, Madrid has a typical **continental climate**, cold and dry in winter, and hot and dry in summer. There are usually two rainy periods, in October/November and any time from late March to early May. With temperatures soaring to over 40ºC in July and August, the best times to visit are generally **spring** and **autumn**, when the city is pleasantly warm. The short, sharp winter takes many visitors by surprise, but crisp sunny days with clear blue skies compensate for the drop in temperature.

Although Madrid is increasingly falling into line with other European capitals, much of it still shuts down in **summer**. For around six weeks from the end of July, many of the inhabitants head for the coast or countryside. Luckily for visitors, and those Madrileños who choose to remain, sights and museums remain open and nightlife takes on a momentum of its own.

◀ Reina Sofía art gallery

literature and the arts flourished with the likes of Cervantes and Goya, centuries of gradual decline and political turmoil followed, leaving Madrid with a slightly parochial image. Following the death of the dictator Franco in 1975 and the return to democracy, however, the city had a second burst of creativity, La Movida Madrileña, and Madrid is now a thriving modern capital.

Millions of visitors head straight for the **Prado**, the **Reina Sofía** and the **Thyssen-Bornemisza**, three magnificent galleries that give the city a strong claim to being "European capital of art". Of equal appeal to football fans is one of the world's most glamorous and successful clubs, **Real Madrid**. Aside from these, there's also a host of smaller museums, palaces and parks which, when combined with some of the best **tapas** in Spain, countless bars and legendary nightlife, makes it easy to see why so many people get hooked when they come here.

Madrid's short but eventful history has left behind a mosaic of traditions, **cultures** and **cuisines**, and you soon realize that it is the inhabitants who play a big part in the city's appeal. Hanging out in the cafés or the summer *terrazas*, packing the lanes of the Rastro flea market, filling the restaurants or playing hard and very, very late in a thousand bars and clubs, Madrileños have an almost insatiable appetite for enjoying themselves. The **nightlife** for which Madrid is renowned is merely an extension of the Madrileño character and the capital's inhabitants

▼ Tapas

▼ Madrid nightlife

consider other European cities positively dull by comparison with their own.

The city centre with its characterful mix of bustling, labyrinthine streets and peaceful squares, punctuated by historic architectural reminders of the past, is in better shape now than for many years thanks to ongoing urban **regeneration** schemes in the older barrios (districts). As with many of its international counterparts, an influx of fast-food and coffee chains has challenged the once dominant local bars and restaurants, but, nevertheless, in making the transition from provincial backwater just thirty years ago to major European capital today, Madrid has managed to preserve many key elements of its own stylish and quirky identity.

▼ Plaza de la Cibeles

Madrid
AT A GLANCE

Plaza Santa Ana

◄ SOL, SANTA ANA AND HUERTAS

The major attraction for most visitors to this, the bustling heart of Madrid, is its beautiful bars and lively nightlife, though the area is also famed for its historic connections with art and literature.

THE PASEO DEL ARTE

Madrid's three world-class art galleries, the Prado, the Thyssen-Bornemisza and the Centro de Arte Reina Sofía, together form what is known as the Paseo del Arte and offer an unmissable attraction for any visitor.

MADRID DE LOS AUSTRIAS ►

Centred around the grandiose Plaza Mayor, Madrid de los Austrias contains some of the most atmospheric parts of the city, a rich array of architectural and artistic treasures – including the lavish Royal Palace – and dozens of great bars and eateries.

The Prado

LAVAPIÉS AND EMBAJADORES

The areas south of Plaza Mayor were originally tough, working-class districts whose character has changed in recent years as the inhabitants become younger and more cosmopolitan, the districts more fashionable, and the bars and restaurants more enticing.

▲ El Retiro

EL RETIRO

The delightful and popular Retiro park is the perfect place to relax and unwind away from the bustle of the city.

BARRIO DE SALAMANCA

Exclusive Barrio de Salamanca contains some of Madrid's smartest restaurants and most of the city's designer shops, and is also home of Real Madrid's Santiago Bernabéu stadium.

◀ Calle Alcalá and Gran Vía

GRAN VÍA

One of Madrid's main thorough-fares and lined with monumental buildings, Gran Vía is also the southern border of Chueca, the focal point of Madrid's gay scene, and bohemian Malasaña, both of which contain an amazing con-centration of bars, cafés, restau-rants and nightlife.

TOLEDO AND SEGOVIA

Two of Spain's most splendid his-toric cities are within easy reach of the capital. Immortalized by El Greco, Toledo remains one of the country's most enchanting places, while Segovia is famed for its fabulous architecture, magnificent mountain setting and outstanding Castilian cuisine.

Ideas

The big six

Madrid's legendary nightlife, multitude of bars and tasty tapas have turned the city into a highly popular weekend-break destination, but as well as eating and drinking, no visit to the Spanish capital would be complete without seeing at least some of the big tourist sights. Three magnificent art galleries, a lavish royal palace, a grandiose central plaza and a colossal football stadium are among the must-see attractions for any visitor.

▼ Museo del Prado

One of the greatest art museums in the world, the Prado contains a fabulous array of work from greats such as El Greco, Titian, Bosch, Rubens, Velázquez and Goya.

P.90 ▶ PASEO DEL ARTE

▼ Museo Thyssen-Bornemisza

An outstanding collection assembled by the Thyssen-Bornemisza dynasty that provides an unprecedented excursion through the history of Western art.

P.93 ▶ PASEO DEL ARTE

▲ Centro de Arte Reina Sofía

An impressive home for Spain's collection of contemporary art, including Picasso's powerful and emblematic masterpiece *Guernica*.

P.94 ▸ PASEO DEL ARTE

▼ Plaza Mayor

Built when the city became Spain's capital in the sixteenth century and once used as a venue for bullfights and executions, Madrid's main square retains an aura of elegance despite the buskers, crowds and somewhat overpriced cafés.

P.51 ▸ PALAZA MAYOR AND MADRID DE LOS AUSTRIAS

▲ Palacio Real

Marvel at the magnificent, over-the-top decor in this one-time royal residence now used only for ceremonial purposes.

P.62 ▸ PALACIO REAL AND ÓPERA

▼ Estadio Santiago Bernabéu

Home to Real Madrid and venue for the 1982 World Cup final, this awesome stadium is a must for any football fan.

P.120 ▸ SALAMANCA AND THE PASEO DE LA CASTELLANA

Kids' Madrid

Children are doted on throughout Spain and the capital is no exception. Kids are welcome at virtually all cafés and restaurants, though you may have to change your child's bedtime schedule if you want to find somewhere for an evening meal. As for sights, Madrid may lack the child-specific attractions of other European capitals, but there's still plenty to keep youngsters occupied and interested during a short stay, from parks and zoos to cable cars and funfairs.

▲ The Teléferico

For a bird's-eye view of the city, take the cable car across the Manzanares river to the middle of the Casa de Campo park.

P.129 ▸ PLAZA DE ESPAÑA AND AROUND

▲ Parque de Atracciones

Of the many rides at this popular theme park, kids will love the white-water rapids ride, the log flume and the stomach-churning La Máquina.

P.131 ▸ PLAZA DE ESPAÑA AND AROUND

▼ Madrid's Zoo

Casa de Campo is home to an attractively laid-out zoo whose child-pleasing animal attractions include lions, bears, koalas, sharks and an extensive collection of reptiles.

P.130 ▸ PLAZA DE ESPAÑA AND AROUND

▲ The Retiro

The large, city-centre Retiro park has, with its play areas, puppet shows, duck ponds and boating lake, enough to allow kids to burn off some excess energy – and plenty of snack bars to refuel.

P.98 ▸ THE RETIRO AND AROUND

▼ Casa de Campo

Wilder and less accessible than the Retiro, the Casa de Campo, with its boating lake, play areas and popular summer swimming pool, is an ideal place to let off steam.

P.130 ▸ PLAZA DE ESPAÑA AND AROUND

After dark

Madrid's renowned late-night scene took off with La Movida Madrileña in the late 1970s when the end of the Franco era released a long-suppressed desire to indulge in pure hedonistic enjoyment. Things have mellowed since, but the city still has a dizzying variety of night-time attractions from chic cocktail spots and cool discobares, to tapas specialists and even a late-night, chocolate-lover's heaven that is a Madrileño institution.

▼ Clubbing

Madrid has a massive range of clubs, from unpretentious discobares to serious cutting-edge dance venues.

P.116 ▸ GRAN VÍA, CHUECA AND MALASAÑA

▼ El Chicote

For a relaxing late-night cocktail, follow in the footsteps of celebrities and try the Art Deco *El Chicote*.

P.115 ▸ GRAN VÍA, CHUECA AND MALASAÑA

▲ Drag queens

Drag queens are a feature of many of the leading Madrid nightspots and for a spot of dinner with your divas, try the popular *Gula Gula*.

P.114 ▶ GRAN VÍA, CHUECA AND MALASAÑA

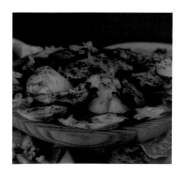

▲ Tapas

Hopping from bar to bar, sampling a variety of tapas, is one of the most enjoyable ways to while away an evening.

P.14 ▶ SOL, SANTA ANA AND HUERTAS

▼ Chocolatería de San Ginés

The traditional way to end a night on the tiles is to have a *chocolate con churros* (thick hot chocolate with deep-fried hoops of batter) at the city's most famous *chocolatería*.

P.69 ▶ PALACIO REAL AND ÓPERA

▼ Santa Ana

Well-established and hugely popular drinking and eating zone around a vibrant plaza. Your only difficulty will be deciding which bar to visit next.

P.88 ▶ SOL, SANTA ANA AND HUERTAS

Green spaces

In complete contrast to its narrow, people-and-traffic-filled streets, Madrid boasts more green spaces than any other European capital. Whether you want a formal English-style garden, a semi-wilderness on the city's doorstep or an indoor rainforest, Madrid provides many welcome escapes from the urban hustle and bustle.

▲ Campo del Moro

One of the city's most beautiful parks is also one of its most underused, but this allows you to enjoy even more the shady paths, ornamental pools and magnificent views up to the Palacio Real.

P.64 ▶ PALACIO REAL AND THE ÓPERA

▲ The Retiro

Once privately owned by the royal family, this city-centre park has become Madrileños' favourite playground, with a boating lake and a crystal palace hosting regular exhibitions among its attractions.

P.98 ▶ THE RETIRO AND AROUND

▼ Jardines Botánicos

Dating back to the eighteenth century, the botanical gardens form an amazingly tranquil oasis alongside the busy Paseo del Prado.

P.100 ▶ THE RETIRO AND AROUND

▲ Casa de Campo

Once part of the royal hunting estate, Casa de Campo is the wildest and biggest of the city's parks, featuring mountain-bike trails, a jogging track, tennis courts and a huge lake.

P.130 ▶ PLAZA DE ESPAÑA AND AROUND

▼ Parque del Oeste

Redesigned after being devastated during the Civil War, the Parque del Oeste contains a pretty ornamental stream, assorted statues, a fragrant rose garden and even a genuine Egyptian temple.

P.129 ▶ PLAZA DE ESPAÑA AND AROUND

▲ Atocha station tropical garden

Contained in an elegant nineteenth-century station and with a constant spray of water enveloping its tropical plants, this garden provides a surreal backdrop to the more mundane activities of this busy railway terminus.

P.102 ▶ THE RETIRO AND AROUND

Shopping

From a ramshackle flea market and eccentric local shops specializing in religious supplies, to food markets and exclusive designer outlets, Madrid provides something for both casual browsers and dedicated shopaholics alike. For fashion, the smartest addresses are in and around Salamanca, while Chueca and Malasaña are the places to go for street wear and shoes. The area south of Plaza Mayor is full of fascinating traditional establishments and antiques can be picked up in the galleries near the Rastro.

▼ Salamanca designer stores

The upmarket Salamanca district is home to some of the city's most exclusive – and expensive – designer outlets.

P.122 ▶ SALAMANCA AND THE
PASEO DE LA CASTELLANA

▼ Calle Postas

For off-beat and eccentric souvenirs, you can't beat the quirky little shops that line the small streets near the Plaza Mayor.

P.53 ▶ PLAZA MAYOR AND
MADRID DE LOS AUSTRIAS

▼ Calle Fuencarral

If the nightlife bug bites and you need the latest fashions to complete your look, Calle Fuencarral is the place to come.

P.111 ▶ GRAN VÍA, CHUECA AND
MALASAÑA

▲ Caramelos Paco

Selling every conceivable type of sugary delight, the only problem you'll have in this old-fashioned sweet shop is knowing when to stop.

P.58 ▶ PLAZA MAYOR AND
MADRID DE LOS AUSTRIAS

▲ Mercados

Even if fresh fish, meat and seasonal vegetables aren't on your shopping list, the city's bustling indoor markets provide a fascinating insight into Madrileño daily life and eating habits.

P.54 ▶ PLAZA MAYOR AND
MADRID DE LOS AUSTRIAS

▼ El Flamenco Vive

All things flamenco from frilly dresses and castenets, to CDs and guitars. A fascinating place to visit even if you have no intention of buying anything.

P.68 ▶ PALACIO REAL AND
ÓPERA

▼ The Rastro

Though better on atmosphere than bargains, it's worth dragging yourself out of bed for the famous Sunday-morning Rastro flea market.

P.71 ▶ THE RASTRO, LAVAPIÉS
AND EMBAJADORES

The big three art galleries

With three celebrated art galleries lying within a kilometre of each other in the city centre, Madrid can justifiably claim to be "European capital of art." The Prado is the top attraction with the Thyssen an ideal complement, while the Reina Sofía is the gallery of choice for those who like their art modern. It would be an impossible task to list all of the museums' highlights, but here are six outstanding pieces, worthy of everyone's attention.

▲ Holbein's Henry VIII

The Thyssen-Bornemisza includes a superlative collection of Renaissance portraits, including Holbein's renowned depiction of the notorious English monarch.

P.93 ▶ PASEO DEL ARTE

▲ Velázquez's Las Meninas

Velázquez's magnum opus has captivated all who have seen it and is rightfully given pride of place in the Prado.

P.92 ▶ PASEO DEL ARTE

▲ Picasso's Guernica

Picasso's masterpiece is the jewel in the crown of the Reina Sofía's collection of contemporary Spanish art.

P.94 ▶ PASEO DEL ARTE

▼ Bosch's The Garden of Earthly Delights

The Prado houses the very best of Bosch's macabre and hallucinogenic work.

P.92 ▶ PASEO DEL ARTE

▶ Goya's Black Paintings

The haunting series of works painted by the deaf and embittered Goya are one of the highlights of any visit to the Prado.

P.92 ▶ PASEO DEL ARTE

Architecture and landmarks

Madrid is home to a hotch-potch of architectural styles reflecting the city's haphazard growth and chequered history. Moorish rule, the arrival of the Habsburgs, the invasion of the French and the Franco dictatorship have all left their stamp on the capital's architecture. There are also a handful of memorable landmarks dotted around the city centre that are worth searching out.

▼ Edificio Metrópolis

The French-designed building at the junction of Gran Vía and Calle Alcalá is one of the city's most stylish constructions.

P.106 ▸ GRAN VÍA, CHUECA AND MALASAÑA

▼ Palacio de Comunicaciones

For sheer architectural extravagance, it's hard to beat the central post office housed in the aptly named Palace of Communications.

P.83 ▸ SOL, SANTA ANA AND HUERTAS

▲ Puerta de Europa

The sloping smoked-glass towers known as the Puerta de Europa provide a dramatic flourish to the end of the Paseo de la Castellana.

P.121 ▶ SALAMANCA AND THE PASEO DE LA CASTELLANA

▼ Atocha

Spanish architect Rafael Moneo did a wonderful job integrating the marvellous nineteenth-century iron and glass railway station into the new terminus for the high-speed AVE trains.

P.102 ▶ THE RETIRO AND AROUND

▲ Plaza de Colón

Cristobal Colón, or Christopher Columbus as he's known to English speakers, is honoured by a monument to him in an eponymous square.

P.117 ▶ SALAMANCA AND THE PASEO DE LA CASTELLANA

▼ Puerta de Alcalá

The huge monumental gate next to the Retiro once marked the eastern edge of the city, and today it's become one of Madrid's most emblematic landmarks.

P.100 ▶ THE RETIRO AND AROUND

Madrid people

Largely a city of immigrants it's difficult to find a person whose real roots are in Madrid, but its status as capital has meant that a string of personalities have made it their home and left their mark on its history, from kings who transformed it into the headquarters of a global empire to movie directors who helped put Madrid on the international map by committing the city's idiosyncrasies to film.

▲ San Isidro

A humble agricultural labourer renowned for his pious devotion and generosity, Madrid's patron saint, San Isidro, is remembered in an annual series of fiestas.

P.56 ▶ PLAZA MAYOR AND
MADRID DE LOS AUSTRIAS

▲ Felipe II

It was Felipe II, Spain's most famous and powerful king, who decided to base the formerly itinerant court in Madrid in 1561, making it the nerve centre of his imperial rule.

P.134 ▶ EL ESCORIAL AND VALLE
DE LOS CAÍDOS

25

▼ Goya

The precursor of modern painting, Francisco de Goya lived and worked in Madrid from the late eighteenth until the early nineteenth centuries, documenting the often tumultuous events played out during his lifetime.

P.92 ▸ PASEO DEL ARTE

▲ Pedro Almodóvar

The enfant terrible of Spanish cinema made his name during the Movida Madrileña in the late 1970s and early 1980s before going on to Oscar-winning success with *Hable con ella* (*Talk to her*).

P.174 ▸ ESSENTIALS

▼ Franco

After his victory in the 1936–39 Civil War, General Franco dominated Spanish life for forty years, running his dictatorship from a residence on the outskirts of the capital.

P.131 ▸ PLAZA DE ESPAÑA AND AROUND

▲ Miguel Cervantes

Playwright, soldier and author of *Don Quixote*, Cervantes lived in the Huertas area and was buried in the convent of Las Trinitarias Descalzas. He is now commemorated by an imposing monument in Plaza de España.

P.126 ▸ PLAZA DE ESPAÑA AND AROUND

Seasonal Madrid

"Six months of winter and three months of hell" is the popular description of the Madrid climate. Temperatures soar in the summer and can drop well below freezing in winter, but contrary to the refrain it is often pleasantly warm in both spring and autumn. Crisp sunny days compensate for the drop in temperature in winter, while open-air swimming pools and outdoor terraces help take the edge off the summer heat.

▼ Swimming pools

There's no better way to cool down in high summer than by heading for one of the city's many open-air pools.

P.175 ▸ ESSENTIALS

▼ Sunbathing in a park

Madrid may be a long way from the nearest beach, but the city's numerous parks provide ample opportunity to soak up some holiday sun.

P.98 ▸ THE RETIRO AND AROUND

▲ Terrazas on the Castellana

Warm summer nights see Madrid's nocturnal life take to the streets with the Castellana a popular venue for trendy outdoor *terraza* bars.

P.125 ▶ SALAMANCA AND THE PASEO DE LA CASTELLANA

▲ Chestnut sellers

Shake off the winter chill with a bag of roast chestnuts, direct from street vendors.

P.173 ▶ ESSENTIALS

▼ La Rosaleda Rose Garden

Spring in the Parque del Oeste means a spectacular display of roses in La Rosaleda.

P.129 ▶ PLAZA DE ESPAÑA AND AROUND

▼ Plaza Mayor Christmas market

The city puts on an impressive light show at Christmas and turns the Plaza Mayor into a massive marketplace selling all manner of festive goods.

P.173 ▶ ESSENTIALS

Eating

Eating out in Madrid is one of the highlights of any visit to the city and there's something to suit every pocket and every taste. From back-street bars to high-class designer restaurants and with a bewildering array of cuisines encompassing tapas, traditional Madrileño, Spanish regional and international dishes, there is no excuse to go home disappointed. In a city that has often been an intimidating destination for vegetarians, there is now a growing number of restaurants offering attractive alternatives to meat.

VERM
YZAGUI
CALAMARES A LA ROM
PATATAS CON TORRE
PULPO A LA GALLEG
MEJILLONES REBO
BOQUERONES EN VIN
SEPIA A LA PLANCHA
CALLOS A LA MADRIL
SURTIDO DE IBERIC
POLLO AL AJILLO
PAELLA DE LA CASA

Vermouth con a

DESDE 1884

▲ Tapas

For an authentic night out eating tapas, forget staying in one place and instead copy the locals and sample the house speciality as you hop from bar to bar.

P.87 ▸ SOL, SANTA ANA AND HUERTAS

▼ La Bola

Established in the late nineteenth century, *La Bola* specializes in the traditional Madrileño speciality *cocido*, a warming and extremely filling meat and chickpea stew.

P.69 ▶ PALACIO REAL AND ÓPERA

▲ Botín

Claiming to be Europe's oldest restaurant, *Botín* is very popular with visitors and deservedly so, given its reputation for serving up excellent Castilian roasts in a cheery atmosphere.

P.58 ▶ PLAZA MAYOR AND MADRID DE LOS AUSTRIAS

▼ El Abuelo

A fabulous little bar serving up a constant supply of fried prawns accompanied by sweet red wine or a cool beer.

P.87 ▶ SOL, SANTA ANA AND HUERTAS

▲ The Museo de Jamón

Packed to the rafters with cured hams, this is an ideal place to sample one of Spain's great delicacies.

P.87 ▶ SOL, SANTA ANA AND HUERTAS

Drinking

Bars and cafés are a central feature of Madrileño life and there's an incredible variety to choose from, including *cervecerías* (beer specialists), *coctelerías* (cocktail bars), *champagnerías* (champagne bars), *tabernas* (old-style taverns), *bares de copas* (bars mainly serving spirits), and, inevitably, a host of Irish pubs. As for coffee, steer clear of the franchised chains and head for a traditional café for a much tastier brew.

▼ La Venencia

A rather dingy-looking bar from the outside, but inside you'll find a wonderful range of Spanish sherries, one of the country's traditional aperitifs.

P.88 ▸ SOL, SANTA ANA AND HUERTAS

▼ Viva Madrid

A classic on the Madrileño nightlife circuit – arrive early to admire the beautiful tiles and vaulted roof before the crowds pour in.

P.88 ▸ SOL, SANTA ANA AND HUERTAS

▼ Drinking granizado or horchata in the Retiro

Granizado (crushed ice with lemon, orange or coffee) and *horchata* (a milky drink made from tiger nuts) are two favourite summer refreshments.

P.98 ▶ EL RETIRO AND AROUND

▲ Coffee culture

There's no better way to kick-start the day than a cup of coffee – or two – at one of the city's traditional cafés.

P.112 ▶ GRAN VÍA, CHUECA AND MALASAÑA

▼ Cocktails at Del Diego

Sample some of the best cocktails in town at this cool and stylish bar just behind Gran Vía.

P.115 ▶ GRAN VÍA, CHUECA AND MALASAÑA

▲ Mariano Madrueño

An old-fashioned wine shop where you can take your pick from the produce of Spain's best vineyards.

P.84 ▶ SOL, SANTA ANA AND HUERTAS

Madrid in a weekend

Madrid is such a compact capital that even in just a couple of days you can sample most of the city's leading sights. No visit would be complete without taking in at least one of the big three art galleries or sampling some tapas. An evening at the football is a further option, while you'll still have time for a visit to the historic centre, some bargain hunting at the Rastro market and a leisurely afternoon stroll around the Retiro.

▲ The Prado

If you have time for just one cultural foray, the Prado, with its superlative collection of fine art, should be it.

P.90 ▶ PASEO DEL ARTE

▲ Tapas

Spend an evening sampling the endless range of tapas on offer in the city's bars.

P.87 ▶ SOL, SANTA ANA AND
HUERTAS

▼ The Rastro

Mingle with the bargain hunters and marvel at what the stallholders are trying to sell at Madrid's rambling Sunday-morning market.

P.71 ▶ THE RASTRO, LAVAPIÉS AND EMBAJADORES

▲ Sunday-afternoon paseo

Join the locals for a Sunday promenade in the Retiro park.

P.98 ▶ THE RETIRO AND AROUND

▲ Football

See Real Madrid's collection of "galactico" superstars at the splendid Bernabéu stadium.

P.120 ▶ SALAMANCA AND THE PASEO DE LA CASTELLANA

▼ Legendary nightlife

If you're eating before 9pm, dancing before midnight and asleep before dawn, you haven't experienced a truly Madrileño night.

P.116 ▶ GRAN VÍA, CHUECA AND MALASAÑA

▲ Plaza Mayor

People-watch over a drink, listen to the buskers or admire the elegant architecture in the city's main square.

P.51 ▶ PLAZA MAYOR AND MADRID DE LOS AUSTRIAS

Sport and culture

Although Madrileños certainly know how to let their hair down, they also have an insatiable appetite for culture and sport. Cinema, *zarzuela* (light opera), classical concerts and flamenco are all firmly established in the capital, while for sports fans two of the country's biggest football clubs have their homes here. For many Spaniards bullfighting is the ultimate spectacle and for those with a genuine interest, Madrid hosts one of the most prestigious taurine festivals every May.

▼ Real Madrid

With nine European Cups, 29 league titles and a myriad other trophies to their name, Real Madrid have the silverware to support their boast to be the greatest club in world football.

P.120 ▶ SALAMANCA AND THE
PASEO DE LA CASTELLANA

▼ Bullfighting

For a few weeks in the year during the prestigious San Isidro festival in May, Las Ventas ring in Madrid becomes the bull-fighting capital of the world.

P.121 ▶ SALAMANCA AND THE
PASEO DE LA CASTELLANA

▲ Atlético Madrid

More down-to-earth than neighbours Real, Atlético are still one of the country's biggest clubs.

P.73 ▸ THE RASTRO, LAVAPIÉS AND AMBAJADORES

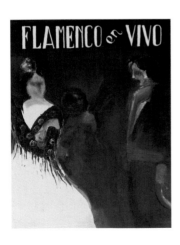

▲ Flamenco

Andalucía may be the home of flamenco, but some of the best acts can be appreciated on the Madrid scene.

P.77 ▸ THE RASTRO, LAVAPIÉS AND AMBAJADORES

▼ Teatro Real

The lavish refurbishment of the nineteenth-century Teatro Real has left the city with a magnificent venue for operas, ballets and classical concerts.

P.66 ▸ PALACIO REAL AND ÓPERA

▼ Cinema

Madrileños are avid movie-goers and the city provides plenty of opportunities to catch Spanish or subtitled foreign films, from blockbusters on the Gran Vía to more specialist offerings at the smaller arthouse cinemas.

P.174 ▸ ESSENTIALS

Specialist museums

Although the big three art galleries dominate the tourist agenda, Madrid is also home to a host of less famous, smaller-scale museums. From fascinating displays on the life of a specific artist or writer to national collections with unique exhibits, these specialist spaces can be just as rewarding as their big-name counterparts.

▲ Casa de Lope de Vega

A delightful little museum set in the reconstructed home and garden of the prolific, seventeenth-century Spanish writer.

P.79 ▶ SOL, SANTA ANA AND HUERTAS

▲ Museo Sorrolla

This atmospheric tribute to the life and work of the artist Sorolla – often called the "Spanish Impressionist" – is housed in his beautifully preserved former residence just off the Castellana.

P.119 ▶ SALAMANCA AND THE PASEO DE LA CASTELLANA

▼ Real Academia de Bellas Artes

It may not be able to boast the heavyweight attractions of the big three art galleries, but the Royal Academy of Fine Art contains some captivating work by Goya, El Greco, José de Ribera and Zurbarán.

P.82 ▸ SOL, SANTA ANA AND HUERTAS

▲ Real Fábrica de Tapices

The Royal Tapestry Factory is both a fascinating museum and a thriving work-shop, allowing visitors the chance to view works in progress and see some of the fabrica's historic finished pieces.

P.103 ▸ THE RETIRO AND AROUND

▼ Museo Lázaro Galdiano

A treasure-trove of paintings, furniture and objets d'art in this outstanding personal collection assembled by publisher and businessman José Lázaro Galdiano.

P.120 ▸ SALAMANCA AND THE PASEO DE LA CASTELLANA

▲ Museo Arqueológico Nacional

The Celto-Iberian bust known as the Dama de Elche is probably the museum's most famous artefact, but it also contains some highly impressive Visigothic, Roman, Greek and Egyptian finds.

P.119 ▸ SALAMANCA AND THE PASEO DE LA CASTELLANA

Out of the city

Madrid has enough attractions to keep you busy for days, but within easy reach of the capital are several alluring sights should you need a break from the big city. Toledo and Segovia, two of Spain's most captivating historic cities, are top day-trip choices, or there's Felipe II's stunning mountain-side palace-mausoleum complex of El Escorial, the riverside oasis of Aranjuez with its lavish Baroque palace, and Franco's former residence at El Pardo to choose from.

▼ Segovia

Segovia is brimming with outstanding architectural monuments including a sumptuous cathedral and remarkable Roman aqueduct.

P.150 ▶ SEGOVIA

▲ Aranjuez

Visit the palace, stroll around the gardens and enjoy the delicious local strawberries at this verdant riverside escape, once a springtime residence of the Spanish royal family.

P.138 ▸ ARANJUEZ AND
         CHINCHÓN

▲ Toledo

With its hill-top location, imposing cathedral and beautiful historical core, Toledo is one of the most dramatic Spanish cities. Try to avoid the summer heat and the weekend crowds though.

P.143 ▸ TOLEDO

▼ El Escorial

Part monastery, part mausoleum and part palace, Felipe II's mammoth construction is the awesome architectural legacy of Spain's most powerful monarch.

P.134 ▸ EL ESCORIAL AND
         VALLE DE LOS CAÍDOS

▼ El Pardo

The royal hunting lodge where Franco had his headquarters contains the Caudillo's old cabinet rooms, the theatre where he used to censor films and the chapel where he prayed.

P.131 ▸ PLAZA DE ESPAÑA AND
         AROUND

Madrid calendar

Madrid has a calendar of celebrations to rival many other Spanish cities. Most events have a religious origin and celebrate some local saint or other, but Madrileños know how to party, and food and drink play an integral part in all festivities. Another bonus is that events are always open to visitors and provide a great way of getting a real understanding of what makes the city tick.

▲ San Isidro

The week-long festivals to celebrate the city's patron saint see music, dance and festivities across Madrid.

P.173 ▸ ESSENTIALS

▼ Christmas

Christmas is a full two-week affair in Spain, ending with a huge procession of the Three Kings in the city centre on the evening of January 5.

P.173 ▶ ESSENTIALS

▲ Carnaval

The pre-Lent blow-out of carnival is celebrated with special enthusiasm in Chueca, but there are costume parades all over the city, finishing off with the peculiar Burial of the Sardine in the Paseo de la Florida.

P.172 ▶ ESSENTIALS

▼ Semana Santa

Though not as dramatic as in Andalucía, Madrid's and Toledo's Easter week processions are still an impressive and moving sight.

P.173 ▶ ESSENTIALS

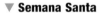

▲ Dos de Mayo

Centred in and around the Malasaña plaza of the same name, these fiestas commemorate the popular rebellion against French occupation in 1808.

P.173 ▶ ESSENTIALS

Gay and lesbian Madrid

Recent years have witnessed an explosion in the gay and lesbian scene in Madrid. The area around Plaza Chueca remains at the heart of the action, but clubs have sprung up in other areas too, and there are plenty of shops, cafés, bars and events catering for the city's gay inhabitants. Once highly conservative, Spanish society now takes a generally liberal attitude towards gay rights and issues.

▼ Plaza Chueca

Centre of the Chueca gay scene, this plaza is always packed with people spilling out from the surrounding bars, restaurants and clubs.

P.107 ▶ GRAN VÍA, CHUECA AND MALASAÑA

▲ Berkana bookshop

One of the best sources of information for all that's happening on the Madrid gay scene.

P.174 ▸ ESSENTIALS

▲ Gay Pride March

Gay Pride Day at the end of June triggers a week of partying, processions and celebrations all around Chueca.

P.173 ▸ ESSENTIALS

▼ Liquid

Stylish bar favoured by an ultra-cool gay crowd.

P.116 ▸ GRAN VÍA, CHUECA AND MALASAÑA

▼ Café Acuarela

Baroque decor, highly drinkable cocktails and a cosy atmosphere make this one of Chueca's most popular cafés.

P.112 ▸ GRAN VÍA, CHUECA AND MALASAÑA

Religious buildings

In a country with such a strong religious tradition it's hardly surprising that the Catholic Church has left its mark on the Spanish capital. Churches, chapels, monasteries and convents pepper the city and, behind often rather modest facades, many conceal remarkable artistic treasures and religious relics. Most places are either free to enter or make a modest charge, but appropriate dress and behaviour are expected.

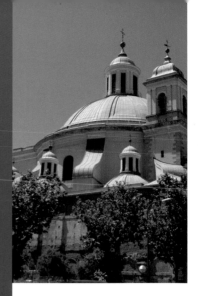

▲ San Francisco el Grande

After a lengthy renovation, the magnificent chapels and frescoed cupola of this enormous church can be seen in something close to their original glory.

P.57 ▶ PLAZA MAYOR AND
MADRID DE LOS AUSTRIAS

▲ Monasterio de las Descalzas Reales

An array of exquisite artworks lies within this former medieval palace that remains a working convent to this day.

P.67 ▶ PALACIO REAL AND
ÓPERA

▼ Iglesia de San Andrés

Badly damaged in the Civil War, much of this church has been restored in recent years, including the fine brick cupola and the richly decorated interior.

P.56 ▸ PLAZA MAYOR AND
MADRID DE LOS AUSTRIAS

▼ Almudena Cathedral

Taking over a century to complete, the city's cathedral is imposing rather than beautiful. Inaugurated by Pope John Paul II in 1993, it was the venue of the recent wedding of heir to the throne Prince Felipe.

P.63 ▸ PALACIO REAL AND
ÓPERA

▲ San Pedro el Viejo

One of the oldest churches in the city, San Pedro features a fourteenth-century Mudéjar tower.

P.55 ▸ PLAZA MAYOR AND
MADRID DE LOS AUSTRIAS

▲ La Ermita de San Antonio

The stunning Goya frescoes that decorate this tiny Greek-cross church provide an appropriate tribute to the artist whose remains are housed within.

P.130 ▸ PLAZA DE ESPAÑA AND
AROUND

Plazas

Madrid has a range of plazas large and small, ranging from the refined elegance of the Plaza Mayor to the down-to-earth cosmopolitanism of Lavapiés. Ideal for a well-earned rest and some Madrileño people-watching, many are also home to excellent bars, *terrazas* and restaurants.

▼ Plaza de la Villa

Madrid's oldest square was once the focus of the medieval city and still houses several local government offices.

P.54 ▶ PLAZA MAYOR AND MADRID DE LOS AUSTRIAS

▼ Plaza Mayor

Brainchild of Felipe II, Madrid's main square has had an eventful, sometimes bloodthirsty history, but today offers an atmospheric backdrop for a relaxing drink.

P.51 ▶ PLAZA MAYOR AND MADRID DE LOS AUSTRIAS

▲ Plaza de Oriente

An aristocratic, tree-lined space, bordered on one side by the Royal Palace and on the other by the Teatro Real and the stylish *Café Oriente*.

P.65 ▸ PALACIO REAL AND ÓPERA

▲ Plaza de España

Big, brash and busy, Plaza de España was part of Franco's attempt to prove that Spain was a modern, go-ahead country by the 1950s.

P.126 ▸ PLAZA DE ESPAÑA AND AROUND

▼ Plaza Santa Ana

Bar-laden square that's the focal point of the Huertas nightlife scene.

P.79 ▸ SOL, SANTA ANA AND HUERTAS

▼ Plaza de Lavapiés

Lavapiés is an animated multicultural barrio with a host of popular bars and cafés.

P.74 ▸ THE RASTRO, LAVAPIÉS AND EMBAJADORES

Places

Plaza Mayor and Madrid de los Austrias

Named after the royal family and their original homeland, the district known as Madrid de los Austrias, or Habsburg Madrid, contains some of the oldest and most atmospheric parts of the city. Centred around the suitably grandiose Plaza Mayor, the area is made up of a twisting grid of streets, filled with Flemish-inspired architecture of red brick and grey stone. Most visitors only make it to the Plaza Mayor and its over-priced cafés and restaurants, but there are appealing sights scattered throughout the area, especially in the characterful barrio of La Latina, which stretches south of the square. This area is also home to some of the city's best restaurants, tapas bars and flamenco *tablaos*, especially around calles Almendro, Cava Baja and Cava Alta.

Plaza Mayor

The splendidly theatrical Plaza Mayor was originally the brainchild of Felipe II who, in the late sixteenth century, wanted to construct a more prestigious focus for his new capital. The **Casa de la Panadería** on the north side of the square is the oldest building, dating from 1590, but, like much of the plaza, it was rebuilt after fires in the seventeenth and eighteenth centuries. The delightful frescoes that adorn the facade were only added in 1992. Today it houses municipal offices and an exhibition centre (Mon–Fri 11am–2pm & 5–8pm, Sat, Sun & hols 11am–2pm; free) displaying temporary exhibits on the history of Madrid.

Capable of holding up to fifty thousand people, the square was used for state occasions, autos-da-fé and executions, jousts, plays and bullfights. The large bronze equestrian statue in the middle is of Felipe III and dates from 1616.

▼ PLAZA MAYOR

PLAZA MAYOR

RESTAURADA

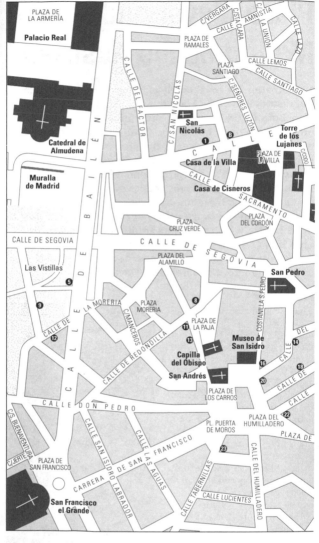

Today, Plaza Mayor is primarily a tourist haunt, full of expensive outdoor cafés and restaurants that advertise themselves as "typical Spanish" – best stick to a drink here. However, an air of grandeur clings to the place, and the plaza still hosts a range of public functions from outdoor theatre and music, to Christmas fairs and a Sunday stamp and coin market.

South of the plaza, the narrow streets hold some of the city's oldest *mesones* (taverns), where an early evening drink allows

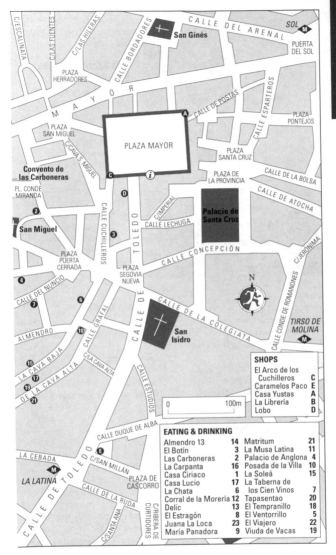

SHOPS

El Arco de los Cuchilleros	C
Caramelos Paco	E
Casa Yustas	A
La Librería	B
Lobo	D

0   100m

EATING & DRINKING

Almendro 13	14	Matritum	21
El Botín	3	La Musa Latina	11
Las Carboneras	2	Palacio de Anglona	4
La Carpanta	16	Posada de la Villa	10
Casa Ciriaco	1	La Soleá	15
Casa Lucio	17	La Taberna de	
La Chata	6	los Cien Vinos	7
Corral de la Morería	12	Tapasentao	20
Delic	13	El Tempranillo	18
El Estragón	8	El Ventorrillo	5
Juana La Loca	23	El Viajero	22
María Panadora	9	Viuda de Vacas	19

you to soak up the atmosphere. Leading off the northeastern corner of the square, Calle Postas is known for its shops selling all manner of religious articles, from dog collars and habits to rosary beads and plastic models of the baby Jesus.

Calle Mayor

One of the most ancient thoroughfares in the city, Calle Mayor was for centuries the route for religious processions from the Palacio Real to the Monastery of Los Jerónimos. The street is home to a variety

▲ PLAZA DE LA VILLA

killing 23 onlookers but leaving the royal couple unscathed.

San Nicolás de los Servitas

Plaza de San Nicolás 1. Sun & Mon 8.30am–1.30pm & 5.30–9pm, Tues–Sat 6.30–9pm. Largely rebuilt between the fifteenth and seventeenth centuries, this, Madrid's oldest church, still includes a twelfth-century Mudéjar tower featuring traditional Arabic horseshoe arches. Inside is a very small but interesting display on the history of Muslim Madrid. Juan de Herrera, architect of El Escorial (see p.134), is buried in the crypt.

of little shops and bars and is flanked by the facades of some of the most evocative buildings in the city. Set back from the road, near the entrance to the Plaza Mayor, is the splendid decorative ironwork of the **Mercado de San Miguel**, built in 1916 and still a thriving market dealing in fish, meat, fruit and vegetables (most stalls Mon–Fri 10am–2pm & 5–8pm, Sat 10am–2pm).

Of Calle Mayor's magnificent early twentieth-century apartment blocks, it's worth stopping off at no. 84, the **Casa Ciriaco**, for a wine or a coffee. This traditional *taberna* is full of memorabilia detailing the colourful history of the building, in particular the notorious attack on the royal wedding procession of Alfonso XIII and his English bride, Victoria Eugenie, in 1906. A bomb, secreted in a bunch of flowers, was thrown from one of the second-floor balconies,

Plaza de la Villa

This charming plaza provides a showcase for three centuries of Spanish architectural development. The oldest buildings are the simple but eye-catching fifteenth-century **Torre y Casa de Los Lujanes** where Francis I of France is said to have been imprisoned in 1525 after his capture at the Battle of Pavia. On the south side of the square is the **Casa de Cisneros**, constructed for the nephew of Cardinal Cisneros (early sixteenth-century Inquisitor-General and Regent of Spain) in the Plateresque style, incorporating the intricate techniques of silversmiths or *plateros* (hence Plateresque). It now houses the Mayor of Madrid's offices.

The remaining side of the square is taken up by the **Casa de la Villa**, one of the most important and emblematic buildings of Habsburg Madrid. It was constructed in stages during the seventeenth century to house the offices and records of the council. The initial design by Juan Gómez de Mora wasn't completed until 1693, 45 years after his death, and was mellowed by the addition of Baroque details in the eighteenth century. The weekly tour (5pm every Mon) is normally only in Spanish but is still well worth it to get a peek inside. The Patio de Los Cristales contains a stunning stained-glass roof depicting some of the city's most celebrated sights, but the highlight of the tour is the Salón de Plenos or Assembly Room, where meetings of the council still take place. The chamber drips with gold leaf and is lavishly decorated with burgundy velvet curtains, red leather benches and frescoes by Antonio Palomino.

Convento de las Carboneras

Plaza Conde de Miranda 3. Founded in the early seventeenth century, this convent belongs to the closed Hieronymite Order. It's famous for the biscuits and cakes it makes and sells – a tradition in Spanish convents since the time of St Teresa of Ávila, who gave out sweetened egg yolks to the poor – that can be purchased every day 9.30am–1pm and 4–6.30pm. Ring the bell above the sign reading *venta de dulces* to be let in, then follow the signs to the *torno*; the business takes place by means of a revolving drum to preserve the closed nature of the order.

Basílica de San Miguel

C/San Justo 4. Mon–Sat 11am–12.15pm & 5.30–7pm. Standing amongst a host of other graceful buildings – most of which house local government offices – San Miguel stands out as one of the few examples of a full-blown Baroque church in Madrid. Designed at the end of the seventeenth century for Don Luis, the precocious 5-year-old Archbishop of Toledo and youngest son of Felipe V, its features include an unconventional convex facade with four recesses, each containing a statue, variously representing Charity, Strength, Faith and Hope.

San Pedro el Viejo

Costanilla de San Pedro. Mon–Thurs & Sat 9am–noon & 5–8pm, Fri 8.30am–9pm, Sun 9am–1pm. Free. At the heart of busy La Latina is the Mudéjar tower of San Pedro El Viejo. The second-oldest church in Madrid, it's said to have been founded in the fourteenth

▼ CAKES FROM LAS CARBONERAS

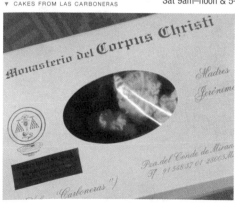

century by Alfonso XI, and stands on the site of an old mosque, though most of the church was rebuilt in the seventeenth century.

Plaza de la Paja

One of the real gems of old Madrid, this ancient sloping plaza was the commercial and civic hub of the city before the construction of the Plaza Mayor, and was once surrounded by a series of mansions owned by local dignitaries. With the restored houses beaming down on the former market square, this is one of the few areas in the city where you can get a break from the interminable Madrid traffic while having a drink at one of several bars. At the bottom is the small Jardín del Príncipe de Anglona (daily: winter 10am–6.30pm; summer 10am–1pm), a survivor of the

▲ IGLESIA DE SAN ANDRÉS

gardens that used to be attached to the nearby mansions.

Iglesia de San Andrés, Capilla del Obispo and Capilla de San Isidro

Plaza de San Andrés. Mon–Thurs & Sat 8am–noon & 6–8pm, Fri 11.30am–1.30pm, Sun 9am–2pm. The Iglesia de San Andrés was badly damaged by an anarchist attack in 1936, and the adjoining Capilla del Obispo is still undergoing a long-running renovation programme. However, the main church, whose brick cupola has been restored to its former glory, and the Baroque Capilla de San Isidro are open to visitors. The chapel was built in the mid-seventeenth century to hold the remains of Madrid's patron saint, San Isidro (since moved to the Catedral de San Isidro), and the interior is decorated with a beautifully sculpted dome, depicting angels laden with fruit. The lower level – inspired by the pantheon in El Escorial, see p.134 – features a red-marble backdrop, fronted by black columns with gold leaf and sculptures of saints.

Museo de San Isidro

Plaza de San Andrés 2 ⓦwww .munimadrid.es/museosanisidro. Sept–July Tues–Fri 9.30am–8pm, Sat & Sun 10am–2pm; Aug Tues–Sat 9.30am–2.30pm, Sat & Sun 10am–2pm. Free. Housed in a reconstructed sixteenth-century mansion – supposedly home to San Isidro – this museum includes an informative exhibition on the history of Madrid from prehistoric times up until 1561 (when Felipe II moved the court here on a permanent basis). The archeological collection is in the basement, while the rest of the building is given over to the saint himself, with displays relating to his life and miraculous activities. It also contains a well that was the site of one of his most famous exploits when he rescued his young son, who had plunged headlong into the deep well, by praying until the waters rose and brought him to the surface again.

The seventeenth-century chapel contained within the museum is built on the spot where the saint was said to have died in 1172.

Parque Emir Mohammed I

Though little more than a scrap of parched land, Parque Emir Mohammed I is notable for its fragments of the city walls that date back to the ninth and twelfth centuries. The park stands next to the Cuesta de la Vega, former site of one of the main entrances to Muslim Madrid, while nearby, the narrow, labyrinthine streets of the former Moorish quarter, La Morería, are still clearly laid out on medieval lines.

San Francisco el Grande

Plaza de San Francisco 11. Tues–Sat: June–Sept 11am–1pm & 5–8pm; Oct–May 11am–1pm & 4–7pm. €3 with guided tour. The huge domed church of San Francisco El Grande has had a varied history. The building was completed in 1784, became a national mausoleum in 1837 and reverted to the control of the Franciscan friars in 1926. Now, after a twenty-year restoration

programme, it's possible to appreciate this magnificent church in something close to its original glory.

Inside, each of the six chapels is designed in a distinct style ranging from Mozarab and Renaissance to Baroque and Neoclassical. Look out for the early Goya, *The Sermon of San Bernadino of Siena*, in the chapel on your immediate left as you enter, which contains a self-portrait of the 36-year-old artist (in the yellow suit on the right).

Even if your Spanish is not that good, follow the guided tour to get a glimpse of the ante-sacristy with its seventeenth-century Plateresque benches carved from Spanish walnut, and the church's art treasures, including paintings by José de Ribera and Zurbarán.

▲ SAN FRANCISCO EL GRANDE

Shops

El Arco de los Cuchilleros

Plaza Mayor 9. Mon–Sat 11am–8pm, Sun 11am–2.30pm. Though at the heart of tourist Madrid, the goods for sale here are a far cry from the swords, lace and castanets that fill most shops in the area. Crafts include ceramics, leather, wood, jewellery and textiles, and there's a gallery space for exhibitions too. Prices are reasonable and staff helpful.

Caramelos Paco

C/Toledo 55. Mon–Sat 9.30am–2pm & 5–8pm, Sun 11am–3pm. A child's dream – and a dentist's nightmare – with a window full of every imaginable sugary confection. Giant lollipops, sugar-coated figures and almond-flavoured sticks of rock are among the delights.

▲ CARAMELOS PACO

Casa Yustas

Plaza Mayor 30. Mon–Sat 9.30am–9.30pm, Sun 11am–9.30pm. Established in 1894, Madrid's oldest hat shop sells every conceivable model from pith helmets and commando berets to panamas and bowlers. There's also a large range of souvenir-style goods, including Lladró porcelain figurines.

La Librería

C/Mayor 78. Mon–Fri 10am–2pm & 4.30–7.30pm, Sat 11am–2pm. Tiny place full of books just about Madrid. Most are in Spanish, but many would serve as coffee-table souvenirs. Also a good place to pick up old postcards,

historic maps and photos of the city.

Lobo

C/Toledo 30. Mon–Fri 9.45am–1.45pm & 5–8pm, Sat 9.45am–1.45pm. Great little shoe shop, selling anything from espadrilles to Menorcan sandals (€24) in every conceivable colour. Particularly good for kids' shoes.

Restaurants

El Botín

C/Cuchilleros 17 ☏913 664 217. Daily 1–4pm & 8pm–midnight. Established in 1725, the highly atmospheric *El Botín* is cited in the *Guinness Book of Records* as Europe's oldest restaurant. Favoured by Hemingway among others, it's inevitably a tourist haunt, but not such a bad one. Highlights are the Castilian roasts – especially *cochinillo* (suckling pig) and *cordero lechal* (lamb). Good house wine too. The *menú del día* is €29.50, but you could eat for less.

Casa Ciriaco

C/Mayor 84 ☏915 480 620. Daily except Wed 1–4pm & 8.30–midnight. Closed Aug. Attractive, old-style *taberna*, famous for its traditional Castilian dishes. The *menú* is €18, main dishes a bit less. You can also sample some of the excellent wine in the front bar.

Casa Lucio

C/Cava Baja 35 ☏913 653 252. Mon–Fri & Sun 1–4pm & 9pm–midnight, Sat 9pm–midnight. Closed Aug. Madrileños come here for classic Castilian dishes such as *cocido* (meaty stew), *callos*

▲ CASA CIRIACO

(tripe) and roasts, cooked to perfection. Booking is essential and count on around €40 a head.

El Estragón

Plaza de La Paja 10 ☎913 658 982. Daily 1.30–4pm & 8pm–midnight. With a fine setting on this ancient plaza, this vegetarian restaurant serves the kind of food that non-veggies also enjoy. It does a varied *menú del día* for €9.50 (dinner *menú* €18), but eating à la carte is a little more expensive. Save space for the desserts.

La Musa Latina

C/Costanilla de San Andrés 12 ☎913 540 255. Daily noon–4pm & 7.30pm–midnight. Stylish restaurant-cum-bar overlooking Plaza de la Paja. Great salads, imaginatively presented tapas and a great wine list, plus an excellent *menú del día* at just €9.50.

Palacio de Anglona

C/Segovia 13 ☎913 663 753. Daily 1–4pm & 8.30pm–1am, Fri & Sat till 2am. Pasta and pizza in a trendy joint, situated in the cellars of an old palace. A handy late-night option, but service can be slow at weekends. Expect to pay at least €25 a head.

Posada de la Villa

C/Cava Baja 9 ☎913 661 860. Mon–Sat 1–4pm & 8pm–midnight, Sun 1–4pm. Closed Aug. The most attractive restaurant in La Latina, spread over three floors of a seventeenth-century mansion. Cooking is typically madrileña, including superb roast lamb and a top-notch *cocido*. Reckon on €45 per person for a splurge.

Viuda de Vacas

C/Cava Alta 23 ☎913 665 847. Mon–Wed & Fri–Sat 1.30–4.30pm & 9pm–midnight, Sun 1.30–4.30pm. Highly traditional, family-run restaurant. The place may look rather down-at-heel, but the good-quality Castilian fare certainly isn't. Great value at around €20–25 per person.

Tapas bars

Almendro 13

C/Almendro 13. Mon–Fri 1–4pm & 7pm–midnight, Sat, Sun & hols 1–5pm & 8pm–midnight. Fashionable wood-panelled bar that serves great *fino* sherry from chilled black bottles. Help yourself to the glasses from the racks on the wall and tuck into original tapas of *huevos rotos* (fried eggs on a bed of crisps) and *roscas rellenas* (rings of bread stuffed with various meats).

La Carpanta

C/Almendro 22. Noon–1am; Mon & Tues opens at 8pm. Lively and very friendly bar just off the Plaza de San Andrés, with a good range of tapas and a cosy brick-lined dining area at the back.

La Chata

C/Cava Baja 24. Daily 2–4.30pm & 8.30pm–12.30am. Closed Tues & Wed lunchtime & Sun eve. One of the most traditional and popular tiled tapas bars, with hams hanging from the ceiling and taurine and football memorabilia on the walls. Serves a good selection of dishes, including *cebolla rellena* and *pimientos del piquillo rellenos* (stuffed onions and peppers).

Juana la Loca

C/Plaza Puerta de Moros 4. Noon–5pm & 8pm–2am. Closed Mon, Sun pm & Aug. Trendy Basque bar serving inventive tapas – *solomillo de avestruz* (ostrich steak) is one of the most popular choices – and very tasty, but fairly pricey, canapés.

Matritum

C/Cava Alta 17. Mon & Tues 8.30pm–midnight, Wed–Sun 1–4.30pm & 8.30pm–midnight. Delicious designer-style tapas, from fig salad with mozarella, anchovies and mint oil to prawn toast with saffron and blackberry sauce. There's an extensive collection of wines too.

La Taberna de los Cien Vinos

C/Nuncio 16. Tues–Sun 1–3.45pm & 8–11.45pm. A vast array of Spanish wines (every month they sell a different selection) plus plenty of tapas to choose from, including excellent leek pie, smoked salmon and roast beef. Not suitable for the indecisive.

Tapasentao

C/Almendro 27. Tues 8pm–midnight, Wed & Thurs 1–4.30pm & 8pm–midnight, Fri & Sat 1pm–1.30am, Sun 1pm–midnight. Fill in a card ticking your choices from the imaginatively presented, very tasty and reasonably priced dishes. Recommended are the excellent asparagus in avocado sauce, *chorizo* with wafer-thin chips, three-cheese salad and *tortilla de bacalao* (cod omelette).

Bars

Delic

Plaza de la Paja 8. Tues–Sat 11am–2am, Sun 11am–midnight. Closed first half of Aug. Serving home-made cakes, fruit juices and coffee, this is a pleasant café by day, transforming into a crowded but friendly cocktail bar by night. There's a good summer *terraza* too.

María Panadora

Plaza Gabriel Miró 1. Tues–Thurs 7pm–2am, Fri & Sat 6pm–3am, Sun 4pm–2am. Closed second half of Aug. An incongruous mix of *champagnería* (champagne bar) and library, where quality *cava* can be enjoyed with the perfect accompaniment of chocolates and mellow jazz – a decadent and highly enjoyable experience.

El Tempranillo

C/Cava Baja 38. Daily noon–4pm & 9pm–2am. Closed two weeks in Aug. Popular little wine bar serving a vast range of domestic wines by the glass. A great place to discover your favourite Spanish *vino* – and the tapas are excellent too.

El Ventorrillo

C/Bailén 14. Daily 11am–1am (till 2am Fri and Sat). This popular *terraza* is good for a relaxing drink while enjoying the *vistillas* (little views) over the Almudena cathedral and the Guadarrama mountains.

El Viajero

Plaza de la Cebada 11. Tues–Sun 2pm–2.30am, Fri & Sat till 3am. Bar, club, restaurant and summer *terraza* all in one, spread over different floors of this fashionable La Latina nightspot. The food (meat, pizza and pasta) is reasonable but it's best to just have a drink.

Flamenco tablaos

Las Carboneras

Plaza Conde de Miranda ☎915 428 677. Open Mon–Sat, shows 9pm & 10.30pm. A relative newcomer to the restaurant/*tablao* scene, geared to the tourist market and slightly cheaper than its rivals, but a good alternative if you want to get a taste of flamenco.

Corral de la Morería

C/Morería 17 ☎913 658 446, ⓦwww.corraldelamoreria.com. Mon–Thurs 8.30pm–2am, Fri & Sat till 2.30am. A good, if expensive, venue for serious flamenco acts, where it's worth staying until late in case there are any spontaneous contributions from the audience. Around €30 to see the show and over double that if you want to dine in the restaurant as well.

La Soleá

C/Cava Baja 27 ☎913 653 308. Mon–Sat 8.30pm–3am. Closed Aug. This long-established flamenco bar is the genuine article. People sit around in the tiny salon, pick up a guitar or start to sing and gradually the atmosphere builds up until everyone is clapping or dancing. Has to be seen to be believed.

▼ LA CHATA

The Palacio Real and Ópera

Although the barrio only became fashionable in the mid-nineteenth century, the attractions found in the compact area around Ópera metro station date back as far as the 1500s. The imposing and suitably lavish Palacio Real (Royal Palace) dominates this part of the city, bordered by the somewhat disappointing Catedral de la Almudena and the tranquil gardens of the Campo del Moro. The restored Teatro Real and Plaza de Oriente have brought back some nineteenth-century sophistication to the area, while the two monastery complexes of La Encarnación and Las Descalzas Reales conceal an astounding selection of artistic delights. For after-dark attractions, two of the city's leading clubs and a handful of pleasant cafés and restaurants are also nearby.

The Palacio Real

C/Bailén ⊛www.patrimonionacional.es. April–Sept Mon–Sat 9am–6pm, Sun & hols 9am–3pm; Oct–March Mon–Sat 9.30am–5pm, Sun 9am–2pm; closed for state occasions. Tours €9, unguided €8, Wed free for EU citizens. The present Palacio Real (Royal Palace) was built by Felipe V after the ninth-century Arab-built Alcázar was destroyed in a fire in 1734. The Bourbon monarch, who had

been brought up in the considerably more luxurious surroundings of Versailles, took the opportunity to replace it with an altogether grander affair. He did not, however, live to see its completion and the palace only became habitable in 1764 during the reign of Carlos III. Nowadays it's used only for ceremonial purposes, with the present royal family preferring the more modest

▼ FORECOURT OF THE PALACIO REAL

Zarzuela Palace, 15 kilometres northwest of the city.

The ostentation lacking in the palace's exterior is more than compensated for inside, with swirling marble floors, celestial frescoes, and gold furnishings filling the rooms. It's a flamboyant display of wealth and power that was firmly at odds with Spain's declining status at the time. Look out for the grandiose Salón del Trono (Throne Room), the incredible oriental-style Salón de Gasparini (the Gasparini Room) and the marvellous Sala de Porcelana (Porcelain Room), decorated with one thousand gold, green and white interlocking pieces.

The palace outbuildings and annexes include the recently refurbished **Armería Real** (Royal Armoury; separate ticket available if you're not visiting the rest of the palace €3.50), full of guns, swords and armour, with such curiosities as the suit of armour worn by Carlos V in his equestrian portrait by Titian in the Prado. Especially fascinating are the complete sets of armour designed for children, horses and dogs.

There's also an eighteenth-century **farmacia** (pharmacy), a curious mixture of alchemist's den and laboratory, whose walls are lined with jars labelled for various remedies.

Jardines de Sabatini

Daily: April–Sept 9am–10.30pm; Oct–March 9am–9pm. The Jardines de Sabatini (Sabatini Gardens) make an ideal place from which to view the northern facade of the palace or to watch the sun go down. They contain an ornamental lake, some fragrant magnolia trees and well-manicured hedges, and, in summer, they're often used as a concert venue.

Catedral de la Almudena

Daily 9am–9pm. Not open for visits during mass: Mon–Sat 10am, noon, 6pm & 7pm, Sun and hols 10.30am, noon, 1.30pm, 6pm & 7pm. Free. Planned centuries ago, Madrid's cathedral, Nuestra Señora de la Almudena, was plagued by lack of funds, bombed out in the Civil War and eventually opened for business only in 1993. More recently it was the 2004 venue for the wedding of the heir to the throne, Prince Felipe, and his former newsreader bride, Letizia Ortiz.

▲ INTERIOR OF LA ALMUDENA

Its bulky Neoclassical facade was designed to match the Palacio Real opposite, while its cold Gothic interior is largely uninspiring. Exceptions include the garish ceiling designs, the sixteenth-century altarpiece in the Almudena chapel and a boutique-like chapel dedicated to José María Escrivá de Balaguer, the founder of the

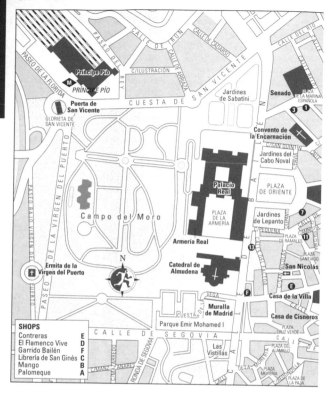

SHOPS

Contreras	E
El Flamenco Vive	D
Garrido Bailén	F
Librería de San Ginés	C
Mango	B
Palomeque	A

controversial Opus Dei religious movement in Madrid. The **crypt** (daily 10am–8pm; entrance on c/Mayor) with its forest of columns and dimly lit chapels is far more atmospheric than the main building.

El Campo del Moro

Entrance on Paseo de la Virgen del Puerto. April–Sept Mon–Sat 10am–8pm, Sun 9am–8pm; Oct–March Mon–Sat 10am–6pm, Sun 9am–6pm; closes occasionally for state occasions. One of the most underused and beautiful of Madrid's parks, the Campo del Moro gets its name from being the site of the Moors' encamp-

ment, from where, in 1109, they mounted their unsuccessful attempt to reconquer Madrid. It later became a venue for medieval tournaments and celebrations. After the building of the Palacio Real several schemes to landscape the area were put forward, but it wasn't until 1842 that things got under way. Based around two monumental fountains, *Las Conchas* and *Los Tritones*, the grassy gardens are very English in style, featuring shady paths and ornamental pools, and provide an excellent refuge from the summer heat, as well as a splendid view of the palace.

EATING & DRINKING

El Anciano Rey de los Vinos	13	Caripén	3
Café los Austrias	11	Casa Gallega	8,14
Café de Chinitas	2	Chocolatería San Ginés	12
Café de Oriente	7	La Coquette	6
La Bola	4	Entre Suspiro y Suspiro	5
El Buey	1	Joy Madrid	9
		Palacio de Gaviria	10

Plaza de Oriente

The aristocratic, pedestrianized Plaza de Oriente is one of the most pleasant open spaces in Madrid. The days when Franco used to address crowds here from the balcony of the royal palace now seem a distant memory, although a small number of neo-Fascists still gather here on the anniversary of his death, November 21.

The showpiece fountain in the centre was designed by Narciso

▼ EL CAMPO DEL MORO

▲ PLAZA DE ORIENTE

Pascual y Colomer, who also transferred the bronze equestrian statue of Felipe IV here from the garden of the Buen Retiro Palace, near the Prado. This statue is reputedly the first-ever bronze featuring a rearing horse – Galileo is said to have helped with the calculations to make it balance. Other statues depict Spanish kings and queens, and were originally designed to adorn the palace facade, but were too heavy or, according to one version, too ugly and were removed on the orders of Queen Isabel of Farnese.

There's a very French feel to the buildings overlooking the square, with their glass-fronted balconies, underlined by the elegant neo-Baroque *Café de Oriente*, a favourite with the opera crowd.

Teatro Real

Plaza de Isabel II ☎915 160 660, box office ☎915 160 606, ticket line ☎902 244 848, ⊚www.teatro-real.com. Open for visits Mon, Wed–Fri 10am–1.30pm, Sat, Sun & hols 11am–1.30pm; reservations ☎915 160 696; €4; tickets on sale from 10am–1pm at the box office. When it opened in 1850, the hulking grey hexagonal opera house became the hub of fash-ionable Madrid and staged highly successful works by Verdi and Wagner. It fell into decay in the late twentieth century and after a ten-year refurbishment – that should have lasted four – and a staggering US$150 million in costs, it finally reopened in October 1997. With its lavish red and gold decor, crystal chande-liers, state-of-the-art lighting and superb acoustics it makes a truly magnificent setting for opera, ballet and classical concerts. Tickets range from €15 to €200, but you'll need to book well in advance for the best seats.

Convento de la Encarnación

Plaza de la Encarnación 1 ⊚www.pat-rimonionacional.es. Tours only (some in English) Tues–Thurs & Sat 10.30am–12.45pm & 4–5.45pm, Fri 10.30am–12.45pm, Sun & hols 11am–1.45pm. €3.60; joint ticket with Monasterio de las Descalzas Reales €6, valid for a week; Wed free for EU citizens. Founded in 1611 by Felipe III and his wife Margarita de Austria, this convent was intended as a retreat for titled women and merits a visit for its reliquary alone – one of the most important in the Catholic world. The solemn granite facade is the hallmark of archi-tect Juan Gómez de Mora, also responsible for the Plaza Mayor. Much of the painting contained within is uninspiring, but there are some interesting items, including an extensive collection of royal portraits and a highly prized collection of sculptures of Christ. The library-like reliquary contains more than 1500 saintly relics from around the world: skulls, arms encased in beautifully ornate hand-shaped containers, and bones from every conceivable part of the body. The most famous of the lot is a small glass bulb said to contain the blood of St Pantaleón – a fourteenth-century doctor martyr – which supposedly liquefies at midnight on the eve of his feast day (July 26). The tour ends with a visit to the Baroque-style church which features a beautifully fres-coed ceiling and a marble-columned altarpiece.

Monasterio de las Descalzas Reales

Plaza de las Descalzas 3 ⓦwww.patri-monionacional.es. Tours only (some in English) Tues–Thurs & Sat 10.30am–12.45pm & 4–5.45pm, Fri 10.30am–12.45pm, Sun & hols 11am–1.45pm. €5; joint ticket with Convento de la Encarnación €6, valid for a week; Wed free for EU citizens. One of the less well known treasures of Madrid, the "Monastery of the Barefoot Royal Ladies" was originally the site of a medieval palace. The building was transformed by Juana de Austria into a convent in 1564, and the architect of El Escorial, Juan Bautista de Toledo, was entrusted with its design. Juana was the youngest daughter of the Emperor Carlos V and, at the age of 19, already the widow of Prince Don Juan of Portugal. Royal approval meant that it soon became home to a succes-

sion of titled ladies who brought with them an array of artistic treasures, helping the convent accumulate a fabulous collection of paintings, sculptures and tapestries. The place is still unbe-lievably opulent and remains in use as a religious institution, housing 23 shoeless nuns of the Franciscan order.

The magnificent main staircase connects a two-levelled cloister, lined with small but richly embellished chapels, while the Tapestry Room contains an outstanding collection of early seventeenth-century Flemish tapestries based on designs by Rubens.

Casa de las Alhajas

Plaza San Martín 1. Tues–Sun 10am–8pm. Free. This three-floored exhibition space, run by local bank Caja Madrid, hosts a range of interesting and well-

▼ MONASTERIO LAS DESCALZAS REALES

presented temporary shows that are usually a cut above many of the others in the city. Recent highlights have included exhibitions on Kandinsky, "Art at the Court of Felipe V" and a series of portraits of the Spanish capital.

Shops

Contreras

C/Mayor 80 ⓦwww
.manuelcontreras.com. Mon–Sat
10am–1.30pm & 5–8pm, Sat
10am–1.30pm. Award-winning guitar workshop, run on this site for over 40 years by the Contreras family, the perfect place for budding flamenco artists to buy the genuine article.

El Flamenco Vive

C/Unión 4. Mon–Sat 10.30am–2pm & 5–9pm. A fascinating little piece of Andalucía in Madrid, specializing in all things flamenco, from guitars and CDs to dresses and books.

Garrido Bailén

C/Mayor 88. Mon–Fri 10am–1.30pm & 4.30–8.15pm, Sat 10am–1.45pm. Comprehensive musical instrument shop, stocking everything from Celtic bagpipes and sitars, to Andean panpipes and drum machines. You can even pick up a bust of John Lennon or Mozart. Worth a browse even if you aren't particularly musically minded.

Librería de San Ginés

Pasadizo de San Ginés. Mon–Fri 11am–8pm, Sat 11am–2.30pm. Second-hand book stall crammed with an eclectic selection of new and old editions, mainly in Spanish but with some English ones too.

Mango

C/Arenal 24. Mon–Sat 10am–9pm. A central branch of one of Spain's most popular chain stores for young women. A wide range of smart and casual wear that won't burn a hole in the pocket.

Palomeque

C/Hileras 12. Mon–Fri 9.30am–1.30pm & 4.30–8pm, Sat 9.30am–1.30pm. A religious department store and the place to come if you want to complete your postcard collection of Spanish saints and virgins.

Cafés

Café de Oriente

Plaza de Oriente 2. Mon–Thurs & Sat 8.30am–1.30am, Fri & Sat till 2.30am. Elegant, Parisian-style café with a popular *terraza* looking across the plaza to the palace. The café – which also houses a presti-

▼ CAFE DE ORIENTE

gious restaurant – was opened in the 1980s by a priest, Padre Lezama, who ploughs his profits into various charitable schemes. There's an equally smart bar, *La Botillería* (open noon–1am, an hour later on Fri & Sat), next door.

Café los Austrias

Plaza de Ramales 1. Mon–Thurs 9am–1.30am, Fri–Sat 9am–2.30am, Sun 9am–midnight. Relaxing old-fashioned café, with marble table-tops and dark-wood interior. Service is slow but it makes a good stop after a visit to the Palacio Real.

▲ CHOCOLATERÍA SAN GINÉS

Chocolatería San Ginés

Pasadizo de San Ginés 11. Mon & Tues 6pm–7am, Wed–Sun 10am–7am. A Madrid institution, this café, established in 1894, serves *chocolate con churros* (thick hot chocolate with deep-fried hoops of batter) to perfection – just the thing to finish off a night of excess. It's an almost compulsory

Madrileño custom to end up here after the clubs close, before heading home for a shower and then off to work.

Restaurants

La Bola

C/Bola 5 ☎915 476 930. Mon–Sat 1–4pm & 9pm–midnight, Sun 1–4pm. Opened back in 1870, this is the place to go for *cocido madrileño* (soup followed by chickpeas and a selection of meats) cooked in the traditional way over a wood fire (lunchtimes only). Try the delicious *buñuelos de manzana* (battered apples) for pudding, and don't plan on doing anything energetic afterwards. Lunch will set you back at least €30. They don't accept cards.

El Buey

Plaza de la Marina Española 1 ☎915 413 041. Mon–Sat 1–4pm & 9pm–midnight. A meat-eaters' paradise, specializing in superb steak that you fry yourself on a hotplate. Great side dishes and home-made desserts, with a house red that's very drinkable, all for around €35 per head.

Caripén

Plaza Marina Española 4 ☎915 411 177. Mon–Sat 9pm–3am. Closed Aug. Quality French restaurant with excellent *magret de pato* (duck) and very tasty sauces, but its popularity with Spanish celebrities means it's overpriced and service can be patchy. Expect to pay around €40 a head.

Casa Gallega

C/Bordadores 11 ☎915 419 055; also Plaza San Miguel 8 ☎915 473 055. Daily 1–4pm & 8pm–midnight. Two airy and welcoming *marisquerías* that have been importing seafood on overnight trains from Galicia since opening in 1915. Costs vary according to the market price of the fish or shellfish that you order. *Pulpo* (octopus) and *pimientos de Padrón* (small peppers, spiced up by the odd fiery one) are brilliantly done and inexpensive, but the more exotic seasonal delights will raise a bill to around €40 a head.

Entre Suspiro y Suspiro

C/Caños de Peral 3 ☎915 420 644. Mon–Fri 2–4.30pm & 9.30–11.30pm, Sat 9.30–11.30pm. Given Madrid's links with Latin America, this is one of surprisingly few decent Mexican restaurants in the city. The food is tasty and the surroundings pleasant, but it is rather cramped and prices are high at upwards of €35 for a meal.

Bars

El Anciano Rey de los Vinos

C/Bailén 19. Mon, Tues, Thurs–Sun 10am–3pm & 6–11pm. Traditional bar founded in 1909, serving good beer, a decent selection of wine and some good standard tapas.

Discobares and clubs

Joy Madrid

C/Arenal 11 ⓦwww.joy-eslava.com. Mon–Thurs 11.30pm–5.30am, Fri–Sun 11.30pm–6am. €12–15 including first drink. This big-name club is home to the thirty-something crowd rather than serious clubbers and is frequented by musicians, models, media folk and footballers. Long queues and a strict door policy, so dress smart to increase your chances of getting in. If you can't, console yourself at the nearby *Chocolatería San Ginés* (see p.69).

Palacio de Gaviria

C/Arenal 9 ⓦwww.palaciogaviria.com. Daily 11pm–late. Nineteenth-century palace with a series of extravagant Baroque salons. A fantastic setting for a late drink, it hosts occasional "International Parties" and dance classes. Entrance €9–15 depending on the night; includes one drink.

Live music

Café de Chinitas

C/Torija 7 ☎915 471 502, ⓦwww.chinitas.com. Mon–Thurs 9pm–2am, Fri & Sat 9pm–3am. Drinks and show €27. One of the oldest flamenco clubs in Madrid, hosting a dinner-dance spectacular. The music is authentic but keep an eye on how much you order as the bill can soon mount up. Reservations essential.

La Coquette

C/Hileras 14. Daily 8pm–2.30am. Closed Aug. Small, smoky basement bar, where people sit in near darkness watching bands perform on a tiny stage. Wednesday and Thursday are blues nights.

▼ JOY MADRID

The Rastro, Lavapiés and Embajadores

Lavapiés and Embajadores were originally working-class, tough districts built to accommodate the huge population growth of the eighteenth and nineteenth centuries. Traditional sights are thin on the ground, but some original tenement blocks survive and the city's former industrial and commercial centre is now famous for the Rastro street market. These barrios are also home to the *castizos* – authentic Madrileños – who can be seen decked out in traditional costume during local festivals. The character of these areas has changed, however, in recent years. Young, trendy Spaniards and large numbers of immigrants have arrived, meaning that Lavapiés and Embajadores are now Madrid's most racially mixed barrios, with teahouses, kebab joints and textile shops sitting alongside some of the most original bars and restaurants in the city. Petty crime can be a problem round here but the reality is not nearly as dramatic as newspapers suggest.

Iglesia-Catedral de San Isidro

C/Toledo 37. Mon–Sat 8am–noon & 6–8.30pm, Sun & hols 9am–2pm & 6–8.30pm. Built from 1622 to 1633, this enormous twin-towered church was originally the centre of the Jesuit Order in Spain. After Carlos III fell out with the Order in 1767, he redesigned the interior and dedicated it to the city's patron, San Isidro. Isidro's remains – and those of his equally saintly wife – were brought here in 1769 from the nearby Iglesia de San Andrés (see p.56).

The church was the city's provisional cathedral from 1886 until 1993 when the new Catedral de la Almudena (see p.63) was finally completed. It contains a single nave with large, ornate lateral chapels and an impressive altarpiece.

El Rastro

Every Sunday morning the heaving, ramshackle mass of El Rastro flea market takes over Calle Ribera de Curtidores. On

▼ FLAMENCO DRESSES IN EL RASTRO

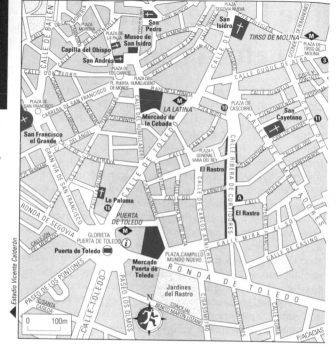

offer is just about anything you might – or more likely might not – need, from second-hand clothes and military surplus items to caged birds and fine antiques.

The area was formerly the site of two large slaughterhouses and the resulting blood that flowed down the hill gave it its name (*rastro* means stain). The establishment of the slaughterhouses acted as a magnet for other traders and craftsmen: tanners – *curtidores*, hence the street name – and food sellers all soon set up here.

Real bargains are few and far between, but the atmosphere is always enjoyable and the bars around these streets are as good as any in the city. Be aware though, that petty theft is a big

problem here, so keep a close eye on your belongings.

Puerta de Toledo

One of several monumental gates that ring the city centre, Puerta de Toledo stands as an eloquent testament to the political vicissitudes of nineteenth-century Madrid. Originally commissioned by Joseph Bonaparte to commemorate his accession to the Spanish throne, the arch ended up being a celebration of his defeat when it was completed in 1827.

Alongside, the **Mercado Puerta de Toledo** was once the site of the city's fish market and now has pretensions to being a stylish arts, crafts and antiques centre, though much of

EATING & DRINKING

Aloque	9	Melo's	13
El Asador Frontón	3	Montes	12
Casa Lastra Sidrería	7	Nuevo Café Barbieri	14
Casa Patas	1	El Sur	6
Los Caracoles (pl/Cascorro)	10	La Sanabresa	2
Los Caracoles (c/Toledo)	16	Taberna de	
Er 77	15	Antonio Sánchez	11
Freiduria de Gallinejas	17	La Ventura	4
Kappa	5	**SHOP**	
La Lupe	8	Galerías Piquer	A

Museo del Ferrocarril ▼

it remains empty, apart from an underused tourist office.

Estadio Vicente Calderón

Paseo Virgen del Puerto 67 ☏913 664 707, ◍www.clubatleticodemadrid.com. Match tickets around €25. Home to Atlético Madrid, one of the city's two big-name football teams, this

▼ LA CORRALA

54,000-capacity stadium makes for quite a sight as its smoked-glass sides rise high above the Manzanares river and the M30 ring road. Atlético may not have tasted the glory experienced by rivals Real Madrid, but the club still ranks as one of Spain's biggest teams and the Calderón is packed with loyal fans for weekend league matches.

La Corrala

C/Tribulete 12 ☏915 309 600. Built in 1839 and restored in the 1980s, this is one of many traditional *corrales* (tenement blocks) in Lavapiés, with balconied apartments opening onto a central patio. Plays, especially farces and *zarzuelas* (a mix of classical opera and music-hall bawdiness), used to be performed regularly in Spanish *corrales*, and the open space adjacent to the neighbouring church usually hosts performances in the summer as part of the Veranos de la Villa cultural programme (see Essentials, p.172).

San Cayetano

C/Embajadores 15. Variable hours, usually daily 9am–12.30pm & 6–8pm.
This remarkable Baroque-style church is dedicated to the patron saint of one of the area's most important festivals (see p.173). José de Churriguera and Pedro de Ribera, both renowned for their extravagant designs, were involved in the design of the elaborately sculpted facade, which dates from 1761. Most of the rest of the church was destroyed in the Civil War and has since been rebuilt.

La Fábrica de Tabacos

C/Embajadores 53. La Fábrica de Tabacos is the oldest tobacco factory in Europe. Originally built as a distillery but modified to produce tobacco in 1809, its austere, unornamented facade is a classic example of early nineteenth-century industrial architecture.

The workforce was overwhelmingly female and constituted, by the end of the century, about twenty percent of Madrid's working population. The flamboyant *cigarreras*, as they were called, were renowned for their independence, solidarity and strength, successfully negotiating with the management for better working conditions.

The building is currently undergoing an ambitious restoration programme with a view to converting it into a new home for the Museo de Artes Decorativas (see p.100).

Plaza Lavapiés

In the Middle Ages, bustling Plaza Lavapiés was the core of Jewish Madrid, with the synagogue situated on the southern side of the square. Today, with its Chinese, Arabic and African inhabitants, it remains a cosmopolitan place, and the plaza, along with the c/Argumosa running off from its southeastern corner, is an animated spot, with a variety of bars and cafés in various states of decay.

▲ PLAZA LAVAPIES

Calle Atocha

Calle Atocha, one of the old ceremonial routes from Plaza Mayor to the basilica at Atocha, forms the northeastern border of Lavapiés. At its southern end it's a mishmash of fast-food and touristy restaurants, developing, as you move north up the hill, into a strange mixture of cheap hostels, fading shops, bars, lottery kiosks and sex emporia. With its brash neon lighting and shiny black facade, the huge sex shop at no. 80, El Mundo Fantástico, stands unashamedly opposite a convent and the site of an old printing house that produced the first edition of the first part of *Don Quixote*.

Cine Doré

C/Santa Isabel 3 ☎913 691 125. Closed Mon. Films €1.35. At the end of the narrow Pasaje Doré alley is the Cine Doré, the oldest cinema in Madrid. Dating from 1922 with a later *modernista*/Art Nouveau facade, it's now the Filmoteca Nacional, an art-house cinema with bargain prices and a pleasant, inexpensive café/restaurant (Tues–Sun 1.30pm–12.30am).

Museo del Ferrocarril

Paseo de las Delicias 61 ☎902 228 822, ⊕www.museodelferrocarril.org. Tues–Sun 10am–3pm. Closed Aug. €3.50. The Museo del Ferrocarril (railway museum) contains an impressive collection of engines, carriages and wagons that once graced the train lines of Spain. The museum, which is housed in the handsome old station of Delicias, also has a fascinating collection of model railways and there's an atmospheric little café in one of the more elegant carriages.

Shops

Galerías Piquer

C/Ribera de Curtidores 29. Mon–Fri 10.30am–2pm & 5–8pm, Sat & Sun 10.30am–2pm. Rather more upmarket than the nearby Rastro flea market, this arcade contains a wide selection of interesting antique shops.

Cafés

Nuevo Café Barbieri

C/Avemaría 45. Daily 3pm–2am, Fri & Sat till 3am. A relaxed, slightly dilapidated café, with unobtrusive music, lots of wooden tables, old-style decor, newspapers and a wide selection of coffees.

Restaurants

El Asador Frontón

Plaza Tirso de Molina 7, 1º (entrance on c/Jesus y María) ☎913 691 617. Mon–Sat 1–4pm & 9pm–midnight, Sun 1–4pm. Charming, old neighbourhood restaurant where locals come for a long lunch. There's a range of delicious Castilian dishes and some fine home-made desserts. Expect to pay around €35 for the works.

Casa Lastra Sidrería

C/Olivar 3 ☎913 691 482. Mon, Tues & Thurs–Sat 1–5pm & 8pm–midnight, Sun 1–5pm. Closed July. Very popular and moderately priced restaurant serving classic Asturian fare: *chorizo a la sidra* (chorizo in cider), *entrecot al cabrales* (steak in a strong blue-cheese sauce), *fabada* (a warming winter stew of beans, *chorizo* and black pudding) and, of course, *sidra natural* (cider). Big portions and at €12.50 the set lunch is very good value.

La Sanabresa

C/Amor de Diós 12 ☎914 290 338. Mon–Sat 1–4pm & 8–11.30pm, Fri & Sat till midnight. Closed Aug. Down-to-earth local restaurant with an endless supply of customers coming for its excellent and reasonably priced dishes. The *menú del día* is €9 and dinner is equally good value. Friendly staff give plenty of advice, but don't miss the grilled aubergines.

Tapas bars

Los Caracoles

Plaza Cascorro 18. Tues–Sat 10.30am–3.30pm & 7–10.30pm, Sun 10am–4pm & 7–10pm. A favourite since the 1940s, this classic bar does a good range of tapas including the eponymous *caracoles* (snails). On Sundays it's always heaving with customers who have worked up an appetite browsing the Rastro.

Cervecería "Los Caracoles"

C/Toledo 106. Tues–Sat 9am–10.30pm, Sun 9am–4pm. Closed July. Another place specializing in snails. A continual supply is served up in a wonderful spicy sauce in this rough-and-ready local bar, all

washed down with the local *vermút del grifo* (draught vermouth).

Er 77

C/Argumosa 8. Daily 1–5pm & 8.30pm–midnight. A small, very popular bar situated in the middle of this pleasant tree-lined street running off Plaza Lavapiés. Excellent *raciones*, inventive salads, friendly service and good wines.

Freiduria de Gallinejas

C/Embajadores 84. Mon–Sat 11am–11pm. Closed Aug. This traditional tiled, family-run bar is famed for serving the best fried lambs' intestines in the city. A variety of different cuts of this very popular and extremely tasty local dish are available as well as straightforward fried lamb.

Melo's

C/Avemaría 44. Tues–Sat 9am–2am. Closed Aug. Standing room only at this very popular Galician bar serving huge *zapatillas* (hunks of bread filled with gammon and cheese) plus great *pimientos de Padrón* and some fine *croquetas*.

El Sur

C/Torrecilla del Leal 12. Tues–Fri 8pm–midnight, Sat & Sun 1–4pm & 8pm–1am. Imaginative and good-value tapas in a friendly bar decked out in posters from famous Spanish films. Popular options are the *ropa vieja* (a Cuban dish made with cuts of beef) and the moussaka. A fine selection of wines too.

Taberna de Antonio Sánchez

C/Mesón de Paredes 13. Mon–Sat noon–4pm & 8pm–midnight, Sun noon–4pm. Said to be the oldest *taberna* in Madrid, this seventeenth-century bar has a

▲ MONTES BAR

stuffed bull's head (to commemorate Antonio Sánchez, the son of the founder, who was killed by a bull) and a wooden interior. Lots of *finos* on offer, plus *jamón* and *queso* tapas or *tortilla de San Isidro* (omelette with salted cod).

Bars

Aloque

C/Torrecilla del Leal 20. Daily 7.30pm–1am. Closed Aug. Relaxed wine bar where you can try top-quality *vinos* by the glass. The tapas, served up from the tiny kitchen at the back, are original and extremely good.

Montes

C/Lavapiés 40. Tues–Sat noon–4pm & 7.30pm–midnight, Sun 11am–3.30pm. Closed Aug. A Lavapiés favourite for those in search of a decent glass of wine and a very tasty canapé. Ask owner César for advice and he'll help find the best ones for you. A great place to start the evening.

Discobares and clubs

Kappa

C/Olmo 26. Tues–Thurs & Sun 8.30pm–2am, Fri & Sat 8.30pm–3.30am. Relaxing chill-out bar, with comfy seats, good music and a mixed gay and straight crowd. DJs get the party started at the weekend.

La Lupe

C/Torrecilla del Leal 12. Daily 9pm–2.30am. Mixed gay, lesbian and alternative bar that has received a recent make-over. Good music, cheap drinks and occasional cabaret.

La Ventura

C/Olmo 31. Thurs 11pm–2am, Fri & Sat 11pm–2.30am. Not easy to find, but this three-floored club is one of the mainstays of the Lavapiés nightscene. Trip hop, dub and drum 'n' bass from top-notch DJs.

Flamenco tablaos

Casa Patas

C/Cañizares 10 ☎913 690 496, ⓦwww.casapatas.com. Shows Mon–Thurs 10.30pm, Fri & Sat 9pm & midnight. €25. Authentic flamenco club with a bar and restaurant that gets its share of big names. The best nights are Thursday and Friday – check the website for schedules.

Sol, Santa Ana and Huertas

The busy transport and shopping hub of Puerta del Sol and the streets around Plaza Santa Ana and Huertas are the bustling heart of Madrid and the reference point for most visitors to the capital. The city began to expand here during the sixteenth century and the area subsequently became known as the *barrio de las letras* (literary neighbourhood) because of the many authors and playwrights – including Cervantes – who made it their home. Today, the literary theme continues, with theatres, bookshops and cafés proliferating alongside the Ateneo (literary, scientific and political club), the Círculo de Bellas Artes (Fine Arts Institute), the Teatro Español and the Congreso de Los Diputados (Parliament). For art lovers, there's the Real Academia de Bellas Artes de San Fernando, an important museum and gallery. For most visitors, though, the main attraction is the vast array of traditional bars, particularly concentrated around the picturesque Plaza de Santa Ana.

Puerta del Sol

This half-moon-shaped plaza, thronged with people and traffic at almost any hour of the day, marks the centre of the city and, indeed, of Spain – **Kilometre Zero**, an inconspicuous stone slab on the south side of the square, is the spot from which all distances in the country are measured. Opposite, near an equestrian bronze of King Carlos III, stands a statue of Madrid's emblem, the **oso y madroño** (bear and strawberry tree).

The square has been a popular meeting place since the mid-sixteenth century, when it was the site of one of the main gates

▼ TIO PEPE SIGN IN PUERTO DEL SOL

into the city. Its most important building is the **Casa de Correos**, built in 1766 and originally the city's post office. Under Franco it became the headquarters of the much-feared security police and now houses the main offices of the Madrid regional government. The Neoclassical facade is crowned by the nation's most famous clock which officially ushers in the New Year: on December 31, Madrileños pack Puerta del Sol and attempt to scoff twelve grapes – one on each of the chimes of midnight – to bring themselves good luck for the next twelve months.

▼ GARDEN IN CASA DE LOPE DE VEGA

The square has also witnessed several incidents of national importance, including the slaughter of a rioting crowd by Napoleon's marshal, Murat, aided by the infamous Egyptian cavalry, on May 2, 1808. The event is depicted in Goya's canvas, *Dos de Mayo*, now hanging in the Prado (see p.92).

Plaza Santa Ana

The main reason for visiting vibrant Plaza Santa Ana is to explore the mass of bars, restaurants and cafés on the square itself and in the nearby streets that bring the area alive in the evenings.

The square was one of a series created by Joseph Bonaparte, whose passion for open spaces led to a remarkable remodelling of Madrid in the six short years of his reign. It's dominated by two distinguished buildings at either end: to the west, the *Reina Victoria*, a giant white confection of a hotel; to the east, the nineteenth-century Neoclassical **Teatro Español**. There has been a playhouse on this site since 1583, and the current theatre is the oldest in Madrid, its facade decorated with busts of famous Spanish playwrights.

Casa de Lope de Vega

C/Cervantes 11. Tues–Fri 9.30am–2pm, Sat 10am–1.30pm (knock if the door is closed). Closed mid-July to mid-Aug. €1.50, Sat free. Situated in the heart of the Huertas district, the reconstructed home of the great golden age Spanish dramatist offers a fascinating glimpse of life in seventeenth-century Madrid. Lope de Vega, a prolific writer with a tangled private life, lived here for 25 years until his death in 1635 at the age of 48. The house itself has been furnished in authentic fashion using the inventory left at the writer's death and highlights include a chapel containing some of his relics, his study with a selection of contemporary books, and a harem. The garden has been replanted and designed according to references found in the writer's correspondence.

Cervantes lived and died at no. 2 on the same street and though the original building has long gone, a plaque above a shop marks the site.

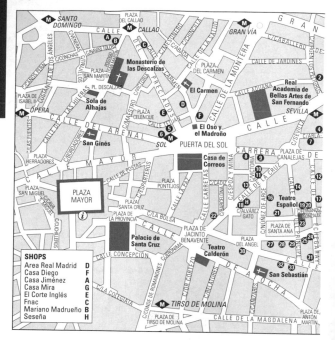

Ateneo Artístico, Científico y Literario

C/Prado 2. Mon–Sat 9am–12.45am, Sun & hols 9am–9.45pm. The Ateneo (literary, scientific and political club) was founded after the 1820 Revolution and provided a focus for the new liberal political ideas circulating at that time. The exterior is Neo-plateresque in style, while the inside features a Neoclassical lecture theatre, a wooden panelled corridor with portraits of past presidents of the club and a splendid reading room. It also has a good-value café.

El Congreso de los Diputados

Plaza de las Cortes ⓦwww.congreso .es. Sat 10.30am–1pm (bring passport). Closed Aug & hols. The lower house of the Spanish parliament meets in a rather unprepossessing nine-teenth-century building. Its most distinguished feature is the two bronze lions that guard the entrance, made from a melted-down cannon captured during the African War of 1859–60.

Sessions can be visited by appointment only, though any-one can turn up and queue for a free tour on Saturday morn-ings. This takes in several of the most important rooms and the chamber itself where the bullet holes left by mad Colonel Tejero and his Guardia Civil associates in the abortive coup of 1981 are pointed out.

Calle Alcalá

An imposing catalogue of Spanish architecture lines Calle Alcalá, an ancient thoroughfare that originally led to the Roman university town of Alcalá de

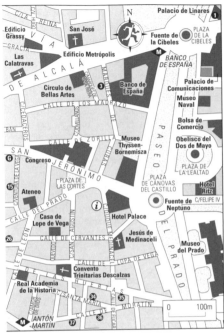

EATING & DRINKING	
El Abuelo	16
Alhambra	10
Arrocería Gala	37
Las Bravas	18
Café Central	30
Café del Español	23
Café Jazz Populart	32
Cardamomo	17
Casa del Abuelo	13
Casa Alberto	33
Casa Labra	5
Cenador del Prado	25
Cervecería Alemana	29
Cervecería Santa Ana	27
Come Prima	26
Domine Cabra	35
La Farfalla	34
La Finca de Susana	7
Hurly Burly	3
El Inti de Oro	15
Las Letras	31
Lhardy	9
La Mallorquina	6
Museo del Jamón	8
Naturbier	28
La Oreja de Oro	11
Paradis erReeFe	1
Prada A Tope	14
Salón del Prado	24
Suite	2
The Room/ Mondo at Stella	4
Torero	22
La Trucha	19
La Vaca Verónica	36
La Venencia	12
Viña P	21
Viva Madrid	20

Henares. Look out particularly for the splendid early twentieth-century wedge-shaped Banco Español de Crédito, adorned with elephant heads and plaques listing all the branches of the bank in Spain; the Banco de

▼ BANCO ESPAÑOL DE CRÉDITO

Bilbao Vizcaya, with its Neoclassical concave facade complete with charioteers on top; and the Baroque Ministerio de Hacienda (Inland Revenue).

Iglesia de San José

C/Alcalá 41. Daily 7am–1.30pm & 6–8.30pm, Sun open from 9am. The red-brick Iglesia de San José, near the junction with Gran Vía, dates back to the 1730s and was the last building designed by the prolific Pedro de Ribera. The interior holds the ornate Santa Teresa de Ávila chapel and an impressive collection of colourful images of Christ and the Virgin Mary.

Iglesia de Las Caltravas

C/Alcalá 25. Mon–Fri 8am–1pm & 6–8pm, Sat & Sun 11am–1pm &

6–8pm. Free. The pastel-pink Iglesia de Las Calatravas was built in the seventeenth-century for the nuns of the Calatrava, one of the four Spanish military orders. Inside, it contains a fantastically elaborate gold altarpiece by José Churriguera.

Museo de la Real Academia de Bellas Artes de San Fernando

C/Alcalá 13 ☎915 240 864. Tues–Fri 9am–7pm, Mon, Sat, Sun & public holidays 9am–2.30pm. €2.40, free Wed. Free guided visits 5pm on Wed, Oct–June. The Real Academia, established by Felipe V in 1744 and housed in its present location since 1773, is one of the most important art galleries in Spain. Its displays include sections on sculpture, architecture and music, some interesting French and Italian work, and an extraordinary – but chaotically displayed – collection of Spanish paintings, including El Greco, Velázquez, Murillo and Picasso.

The Goya section has two revealing self-portraits, several depictions of the despised royal favourite *Don Manuel Godoy*, the desolate representation of *The Madhouse*, and *The Burial of the Sardine* (a popular procession that continues to this day in Madrid).

The gallery is also home to the national chalcography collection (Mon–Fri 10am–2pm, Sat 10am–1.30pm; free), which includes some Goya etchings and several of the copper plates used for his *Capricho* series on show in the Prado.

Note that staff shortages often cause gallery closures and there are frequent changes to the opening hours, so it pays to check before you visit.

Círculo de Bellas Artes

C/Marqués de Casa Riera 2. Exhibitions Tues–Fri 5–9pm, Sat 11am–2pm & 5–9pm, Sun 11am–2pm. €0.60, €1 after 4pm. This striking 1920s Art Deco building, crowned by a statue of Pallas Athene, is home to one of Madrid's best arts centres. Inside there's a theatre, music hall, exhibition galleries, cinema and a very relaxing café-bar (see p.88).

For many years a stronghold of Spain's intelligentsia, it attracts the city's arts and media crowd but is not exclusive, nor expensive. As the Círculo is theoretically a members-only club, it issues day membership on the door, for which you get access to all areas.

▼ CAFÉ IN BELLAS ARTES

Plaza de la Cibeles

Encircled by four of the most monumental buildings in Madrid – the Palacio de Comunicaciones (the Post Office), Banco de España (the Central Bank), the Palacio de

▲ PLAZA DE LA CIBELES

Buenavista (the Army HQ) and the Palacio de Linares (the Casa de América) – Plaza de la Cibeles is one of the city's most famous landmarks. At its centre, and marooned in a sea of never-ending traffic, is the late eighteenth-century fountain and statue of the goddess Cibeles, riding in a chariot drawn by two lions. Built to celebrate the city's first public water supply, today the fountain sees celebrations of a different kind as the favoured location for Real Madrid fans to congregate after a victory (Atlético supporters bathe in the fountain of Neptune just down the road).

Palacio de Comunicaciones

This grandiose wedding-cake of a building, constructed between 1904 and 1917, is Madrid's main post office. Much more imposing than the parliament, the exterior is flanked by polished brass postboxes for each province, while the interior preserves a totally Byzantine system, with scores of counters each offering a particular service, from telegrams to string. To the rear of the building is a small museum (Mon–Fri 9am–2pm & 5–7pm, Sat 9am–2pm, free; entry on c/Montalbán) detailing the history of the postal service and communications.

Palacio de Linares

ⓦwww.casamerica.es. Tues–Sat 11am–7pm, Sun 11am–2pm. This palatial eighteenth-century mansion, built by the Marqués de Linares, is now home to the Casa de América, a cultural organization that promotes Latin American art through an ambitious programme of concerts, films and exhibitions. It also has a good bookshop, a fine restaurant (see p.86) and an excellent summer garden terrace.

Shops

Area Real Madrid

C/Carmen 3. Mon–Sat 10am–9pm, Sun 11am–8pm. Newly opened club store where you can pick up replica shirts and all manner of – expensive – souvenirs related to the club's history. There are smaller branches in the shopping centre on the corner of

Real's Bernabéu stadium at c/Concha Espina 1 and at Gate 3 of the stadium itself.

Casa Diego
Puerta del Sol 12. Mon–Sat 9.30am–8pm. Old-fashioned shop with helpful staff selling a fantastic array of Spanish fans (*abanicos*) ranging from cheap offerings at under €5 to beautifully hand-crafted works of art costing up to €200. Sells umbrellas and walking sticks too.

Casa Jiménez
C/Preciados 42. Mon–Sat 10am–1.30pm & 5–8pm, closed Sat pm in July and all day Sat in Aug. One of the oldest shops in Spain, where you can buy elaborately embroidered *mantones* (shawls) made in Seville, with prices from €100 to €600, as well as gorgeous fans from around €40.

Casa Mira
Carrera de San Jerónimo 30. Daily 10am–2pm & 5–9pm. The place to go for *turrón* (flavoured nougat, eaten by nearly all Spaniards at Christmas) and marzipan. The family business has been open for almost a hundred and fifty years since the founder, Luis Mira, arrived from Asturias and set up a stall in Puerta del Sol.

El Corte Inglés
C/Preciados 1–4. Mon–Sat 10am–9pm & first Sunday in the month. The Spanish department store *par excellence*. It's not cheap, but the quality is very good, plus the staff are highly professional (the majority speak English) and there's a classy food department too.

Fnac
C/Preciados 28. Metro Callao. Mon–Sat 10am–9.30pm, Sun noon–9.30pm. French department store with excellent sections for books, videos, CDs and electrical equipment. Also sells concert tickets.

Mariano Madrueño
C/Postigo San Martín 3. Mon–Fri 9.30am–2pm & 5–8pm, Sat 9.30am–2pm. Great traditional wine seller's, established back in 1895, where there's an overpowering smell of grapes as you peruse its vintage-crammed shelves. Intriguing tipples include powerful Licor de Hierbas from Galicia and homemade Pacharán (aniseed liqueur with sloe berries).

▲ THE BEAR AND STRAWBERRY TREE – MADRID'S EMBLEM

Seseña
C/Cruz 23. Mon–Sat 10am–1.30pm & 4.30–8pm. Open since 1901, this shop specializes in traditional Madrileño capes for royalty and celebrities. Clients have included Luis Buñuel, Gary Cooper and Hillary Clinton.

Cafés

Café del Español

C/Príncipe 25. Mon–Sat 9.30am–3am, Sun 9–30am–1am This tasteful café makes for a relaxing stop on an afternoon sightseeing tour or a late-night bar crawl. Cocktails and snacks served too.

La Mallorquina

Puerta del Sol 2. Daily 8am–9pm. Classic Madrid café, good for breakfast or snacks. Try one of their *napolitanas* (cream slices) in the sunny upstairs salon that overlooks Puerta del Sol.

Salón del Prado

C/Prado 4. Mon & Tues 2pm–midnight, Wed–Sun 2pm–2am. Elegant Parisian-style café-bar serving great coffee and hosting classical music on Thursday nights at 11pm. Turn up early if you want a table.

Restaurants

Arrocería Gala

C/Moratín 22 ☎914 292 562. Daily 1–5pm & 9pm–1.30am. Fantastic-value restaurant specializing in paellas and *fideuás* (paella made with noodles instead of rice). Book ahead and avoid weekends when the crowds mean that the food isn't always up to standard. No cards accepted, but it will only cost you around €20 per head.

El Cenador del Prado

C/Prado 4 ☎914 291 561. Mon–Fri 1.30–4pm & 9pm–midnight, Sat 9pm–midnight. Closed Aug. Relaxing, stylish decor and imaginative cuisine here, combining Spanish, Mediterranean and Far Eastern influences. There's a *menú de degustación* at €35 and some spectacular desserts.

Come Prima

C/Echegaray 27 ☎914 203 042. Mon 9pm–midnight, Tues–Sat 1.30–4pm & 9pm–midnight. Closed Aug. Superior Italian restaurant, with fresh ingredients, excellent antipasti and authentic main courses including a great seafood risotto. Very popular so make sure you book, and expect to pay €28–35 a head.

Domine Cabra

C/Huertas 54 ☎914 294 365. Mon–Sat 2–4pm & 9–11.30pm, Sun 2–4pm. Closed Sat lunch & Sun in Aug and first half of Sept. Interesting mix of traditional and modern, with *madrileña* standards given the *nueva cocina* (new cuisine) treatment. Tasty sauces – a rarity in Spain – and nice presentation too. Very good-value *menús* at €18 & €24 and friendly service.

La Farfalla

C/Santa María 17 ☎913 694 691. Open 9pm to late (4am at weekends). The place to go for late-night food and a lively party atmosphere. The good range of tasty pizzas and Argentinian-style meat will set you back less than €20 a head.

La Finca de Susana

C/Arlabán 4. Daily 1–3.45pm & 8.30–11.45pm. One of two great-value restaurants set up by a group of Catalan friends (the other is *La Gloria de Montera* just off Gran Vía, see p.114). Great *menú del día* for around €8, consisting of simple dishes cooked with imagination. Stylish decor and quick, efficient service too, but arrive early to avoid queuing, as you can't book.

Hurly Burly

C/Marqués de Cubas 2 ☎915 232 367.
1.30–4pm & 9pm–12.30am.
Culinary bright ideas to match
the decor at this new restaurant.
The lunchtime menu is excellent value at €10.50 and features an imaginative selection of
dishes, including a vegetarian
option. An evening meal is
around €30 including wine.

El Inti de Oro

C/Ventura de la Vega 12 ☎914 296
703. Daily 1.30–4pm & 8.30pm–midnight. Also at c/Amor de Dios 9 ☎914
291 958. The friendly staff at this
good-value Peruvian restaurant
are more than ready to provide
suggestions for those new to the
cuisine. The *pisco sour*, a cocktail
of Peruvian liquor, lemon juice,
egg white and sugar is a recommended starter, while the *cebiche
de merluza* (raw fish marinated
in lemon juice) is a wonderful
dish. A full meal costs around
€25.

Las Letras

C/Echegaray 26 ☎914 291 206. Closed
Mon & second half of Aug. Small
informal bar/restaurant with
designerish touches to the decor
and food. The constantly changing set menu usually contains a
good selection of healthy and
very tasty options at a competitive €8.50 (available Mon–Sat).

Lhardy

Carrera de San Jerónimo 8 ☎915 213
385. Shop: Mon–Sat 9.30am–3pm &
5–9.30pm, Sun 9am–2.30pm.
Restaurant: Mon–Sat 1–3.30pm &
9–11.30pm, Sun 1–3.30pm. Once
the haunt of royalty, this is one
of Madrid's most beautiful and
famous restaurants. It's greatly
overpriced – expect to pay over
€45 per head for a three-course
meal – but on the ground floor,
there's a wonderful bar/shop

where you can snack on
canapés, *fino* and *consommé*,
without breaking the bank.

Paradis erReeFe

Palacio de Linares, Paseo de Recoletos
2 ☎915 754 540. 1–4pm and
9pm–midnight. Closed Sat lunch, Sun
& Aug. This place has a wonderful
setting in the Palacio de Linares,
and specializes in Mediterranean
rice dishes. Try the wonderful
arroz negro with seafood and
expect to pay around €35 a
head. The original branch is
nearby at c/Marqués de Cubas
14 (☎914 297 303).

Prada A Tope

C/Príncipe 11 ☎914 295 921.
Tues–Sun 12.30–5pm & 8pm–midnight. Quality produce from the
El Bierzo region of León. The
morcilla (black pudding), *empa-
nada* (pasty) and *tortilla* are
extremely tasty, while the
smooth house wines provide the
ideal accompaniment.

Suite

C/Virgen de los Peligros 4. Mon–Sat
1.30–4.30pm & 9pm–2.30am. Stylish
restaurant serving an imaginative
€10 set lunch and an excellent
€25 *menú de degustación* for dinner, often with good vegetarian
options. In the evening, the
front area becomes a cocktail
bar and is a great place to start
off a night on the tiles.

La Vaca Verónica

C/Moratín 38 ☎914 297 827. Mon–Fri
2–4pm & 9pm–midnight, Sat 9pm–
midnight. A wide range of dishes
is available at this amiable little
restaurant, from great Argentinian-style meat and fresh pasta in
imaginative sauces, to quality
fish and tasty vegetables. Try the
Filet Verónica and the *carabinero
con pasta*. The *menú del día* is a
reasonable €13.50.

Tapas bars

El Abuelo

C/Núñez de Arce 3. Wed–Sun 11.30am–3.30pm & 6.30–11.30pm. There's a *comedor* at the back of this inexpensive bar, where you can order a selection of traditional *raciones* – the *croquetas* are especially good – and a jug of house wine.

Las Bravas

C/Alvarez Gato 3. Other branches at c/Espoz y Mina 13 and Pasaje Mathéu. Daily noon–4pm and 7pm–midnight. Standing-room only at these three bars, where, as the name suggests, *patatas bravas* are the thing to try. In fact, *Las Bravas* has patented its own version of the spicy sauce.

▲ CASA DEL ABUELO

Casa del Abuelo C/Victoria 12.

Daily 11.30am–3.30pm & 6.30–11.30pm. A tiny, highly atmospheric bar serving just their own sweet red wine and cooked prawns – try them *al ajillo* (in garlic) or *a la plancha* (fried). Use your free wine voucher to get a drink at the nearby sister bar, *El Abuelo* (see p.87).

Casa Alberto

C/Huertas 18 ☎914 299 356. Tues–Sat 8am–2am, Sun noon–4pm. Traditional *tasca* with a zinc and marble bar that has resisted the passage of time since it was founded back in 1827. Good *caracoles* (snails), *gambas* (prawns) and a great anchovy canapé, ideally accompanied by a glass of house vermouth.

Casa Labra

C/Tetuán 12 ☎915 310 081. Mon–Sat 11am–3.30pm & 5.30–11pm. Dating from 1869 – and where the Spanish Socialist Party was founded ten years later – this traditional and highly popular place retains much of its original interior. Order a drink at the bar and a *ración* of *bacalao* (cod fried in batter) or some of the best *croquetas* in town. There's also a restaurant at the back serving classic Madrileño food.

Museo del Jamón

Carrera de San Jerónimo 6. Mon–Sat 9am–midnight, Sun 10am–midnight. The largest branch of this Madrid chain, from whose ceilings are suspended hundreds of *jamones* (hams). The best – and they're not cheap – are the *jabugos* from the Sierra Morena, though a filling ham sandwich is only around €5.

La Oreja de Oro

C/Victoria 9. May–July & Sept Mon–Sat 1–4pm & 8pm–1am; Oct–April Tues–Sun 1–4pm & 8pm–1am. Closed Aug. Standing room only in this spit-and-sawdust bar. Try the excellent *pulpo a la Gallega* (sliced octopus served on a bed of potatoes seasoned with cayenne pepper) washed down with Ribeiro wine. Plenty of other seafood tapas on offer too.

La Trucha

C/Manuel Fernández y González 3 ☎914 295 833. Branch at nearby c/Nuñez de Arce 6 ☎915 320 890.

Closed Sun. Ever popular and usually crowded tapas bar cum moderately priced restaurant, where smoked fish and *pimientos de Padrón* are the specialities.

Viña P

Plaza de Santa Ana 3. Daily 1–4pm & 8pm–12.30am. Very friendly staff serving a great range of tapas in a bar decked out with bullfighting paraphernalia. Try the asparagus, stuffed mussels and the mouthwatering *almejas a la marinera* (clams in a garlic and white wine sauce).

Bars

Alhambra

C/Victoria 9. Daily noon–2am. A friendly tapas bar by day, *Alhambra* transforms itself into a fun disco bar by night with the crowds spilling over into the *El Buscón* bar next door.

Cervecería Alemana

Plaza de Santa Ana 6. Mon & Wed–Sun 10am–12.30am, Fri & Sat till 2am. Refurbished but still stylish old beer house, once frequented by Hemingway. Order a *caña* (draught beer) and go easy on the tapas, as the bill can mount up fast.

▼ BAR IN PLAZA SANTA ANA

Cervecería Santa Ana

Plaza de Santa Ana 10. Daily 11am–1.30am, Fri & Sat till 2.30am. Cheaper than the *Alemana*, with tables outside, and offering quality beer, friendly service, and a good selection of tapas. Always packed at night.

Círculo de Bellas Artes

C/Alcalá 42. Daily 8am–2am, Fri & Sat till 3am. A luxurious bar in this classy arts centre, complete with reclining nude sculpture, chandeliers and sofas, and a pleasant lack of pretensions. Service can be slow though. From May to October there's a comfortable *terraza* outside.

Naturbier

Plaza de Santa Ana 9. Daily 8pm–3am. Try this place's own tasty beer with a variety of German sausages to accompany it. There's usually room to sit in the cellar down below if the top bar is too crowded.

La Venencia

C/Echegaray 7. Daily 7.30pm–1.30am. Closed Aug. Rather dilapidated, wooden-panelled bar that's great for sherry sampling. The whole range is here, served from wooden barrels, and accompanied by delicious olives and *mojama* (dry salted tuna). Atmospheric and authentic.

Viva Madrid

C/Manuel Fernández y González 7. Daily noon–2am, Fri & Sat till 3am. A fabulous tiled bar – both outside and in – offering cocktails, beer and speciality coffees, plus basic tapas. Get here

▲ LIVELY HUERTAS

Torero

C/Cruz 26. Tues–Sat 11pm–5.30am (4.30am Wed). Very popular and enjoyable two-floored club right in the heart of the Santa Ana area. No entry fee, but bouncers are pretty strict and you have to be reasonably well dressed to get in.

Live music

Café Central

Plaza del Ángel 10 ☎913 694 143. Mon–Sat noon–1.30am, Fri & Sat till 2.30am. €9–11 for gigs, otherwise free. Small and relaxed jazz club that gets the odd big name, plus strong local talent. The Art Deco café is worth a visit in its own right.

Café Jazz Populart

C/Huertas 22 ☎914 298 407. Daily 6pm–2.30am; live music supplement €6. Another friendly and laid-back venue, with twice-nightly sets (11pm & 12.30am) from jazz and blues bands.

Cardamomo

C/Echegaray 15. Daily 9pm–4am. Noisy and fun flamenco bar with a jam session every Wednesday at 10.30pm in an unpretentious atmosphere that couldn't be more different from the formal *tablaos*. No entry charge and drinks are standard prices.

early if you want to see the tiles in their full glory, as it gets very crowded. Quite pricey, but certainly worth a stop.

Discobares and clubs

The Room/Mondo at Stella

C/Arlabán 7. Thurs–Sat 1–6am. Entrance €9–11 including first drink. Now unrecognisable from its days as a *Movida* classic, *Stella* has undergone a complete makeover to become a cool modern club with transparent dance floor. It remains a big favourite with the city's serious party-goers, especially for the *Room* sessions on Fridays and Saturdays.

The Paseo del Arte

Madrid's three world-class art galleries are all located within a kilometre of each other along what is commonly known as the Paseo del Arte.

The Prado is the main attraction, housing an unequalled display of Spanish art, an outstanding Flemish collection and an impressive assemblage of Italian work. The Thyssen-Bornemisza, based on one of the world's greatest private art collections, provides an excursion through Western art from the fourteenth to the late twentieth centuries, excelling in all the areas in which the Prado is deficient. The final member of the trio, the Centro de Arte Reina Sofía, is an immense exhibition space, home to the Spanish collection of contemporary art, including the Miró and Picasso legacies and the jewel in the crown – Guernica.

If you're planning to visit all three galleries then pick up the Paseo del Arte ticket for €7.66 from any of the three. For souvenirs, each museum has excellent shops selling a range of gifts connected to both their own collections and to art in general.

Museo del Prado

ⓦmuseoprado.mcu.es. Tues–Sun 9am–7pm, hols 9am–2pm. €3, free on Sun and for under-18s and over-65s. The Prado is Madrid's premier tourist attraction and one of the oldest and greatest collections of art in the world, largely amassed by the Spanish royal family – for the most part discerning and avid buyers – over the last two hundred years. Finding enough space for displaying the works has always been a problem but a controversial 43 million-euro **modernization plan**, which

Las Meninas

One of the Prado's most-prized treasures, Velázquez's *Las Meninas* has been admired by public and artists alike since it was completed in 1656. Manet remarked of it, "After this I don't know why the rest of us paint"; the French poet Gautier asked, "But where is the picture?" because it seemed to him a continuation of the room; while the Italian painter, Luca Giordano, identified it as "the Theology of Painting".

Velázquez's skill as a portraitist had been recognised in 1623 when he was made court artist and established himself in Madrid. Painted more than thirty years later, his most famous work captures a moment in the artist's study, featuring Velázquez himself, the Infanta Margarita, various royal attendants, and Felipe IV and his wife, Mariana of Austria – standing in the viewer's position – reflected in the mirror on the wall. The artist's superlative brushwork and his mastery of colour, light and perspective mark the piece out as one of the all-time great works of art and secure Velázquez's reputation as Spain's most accomplished painter.

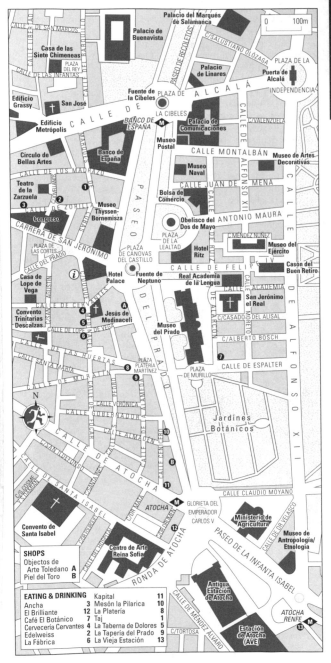

0   100m

Palacio del Marqués de Salamanca
Palacio de Buenavista
C/SALUSTIANO OLOZAGA
CALLE DE SAN MARCOS
Casa de las Siete Chimeneas
PLAZA DEL REY
CALLE DE LAS INFANTAS
PLAZA DE LA
PLAZA DE LA INDEPENDENCIA
Puerta de Alcalá
Palacio de Linares
Edificio Grassy
San José
CALLE DE ALCALÁ
Fuente de la Cibeles
PLAZA DE LA CIBELES
Edificio Metrópolis
CALLE DE ALCALÁ
C/VALENZUELA
Banco de España
Palacio de Comunicaciones
CALLE DE ALFONSO XI
Círculo de Bellas Artes
Banco de España
Museo Postal
CALLE MONTALBÁN
Museo de Artes Decorativas
CALLE DE LOS MADRAZO
Teatro de la Zarzuela
Museo Naval
CALLE JUAN DE MENA
CALLE DE ZORRILLA
Museo Thyssen-Bornemisza
Bolsa de Comercio
ANTONIO MAURA
Congreso
CARRERA DE SAN JERÓNIMO
Obelisco del Dos de Mayo
C. MÉNDEZ NÚÑEZ
PLAZA DE LAS CORTES
PLAZA DE LA LEALTAD
Museo del Ejército
PLAZA DE CÁNOVAS DEL CASTILLO
Hotel Ritz
CALLE DE FELIPE IV
Casón del Buen Retiro
Casa de Lope de Vega
Hotel Palace
Fuente de Neptuno
Real Academia de la Lengua
CALLE ACADEMIA
Convento Trinitarias Descalzas
CALLE DE CERVANTES
Jesús de Medinaceli
San Jerónimo el Real
C/CASADO DEL ALISAL
CALLE DE LOPE DE
CALLE DE LAS HUERTAS
Museo del Prado
C/ALBERTO BOSCH
CALLE SANTA MARÍA
PLAZA PLATERÍA MARTÍNEZ
PLAZA DE MURILLO
CALLE DE ESPALTER
CALLE VERÓNICA
CALLE GOBERNADOR
Jardines Botánicos
CALLE DE ATOCHA
CALLE DE JUAN ILDEFONSO
CALLE ALMADÉN
CALLE CLAUDIO MOYANO
C/SANTA ISABEL
C/COSME Y DAMIÁN
Convento de Santa Isabel
ATOCHA
GLORIETA DEL EMPERADOR CARLOS V
Ministerio de Agricultura
Museo de Antropología/Etnología
CALLE DE DR VELASCO
CALLE DE ALFONSO XII
PASEO DE RECOLETOS
PASEO DEL PRADO
PASEO DE LA INFANTA ISABEL
Centro de Arte Reina Sofía
RONDA DE ATOCHA
Antigua Estación de Atocha
CALLE DE MÉNDEZ ÁLVARO
C/TORTOSA
Estación de Atocha (AVE)
ATOCHA RENFE

N

SHOPS
Objectos de Arte Toledano   A
Piel del Toro   B

EATING & DRINKING		Kapital	11
Ancha	3	Mesón la Pilarica	10
El Brillante	12	La Platería	8
Café El Botánico	7	Taj	1
Cervecería Cervantes	4	La Taberna de Dolores	5
Edelweiss	2	La Tapería del Prado	9
La Fábrica	6	La Vieja Estación	13

includes a new glass-fronted building on the site of San Jerónimo church's eighteenth-century cloisters, is due to be completed in 2005 and will enable the Prado to double the number of paintings on show.

There are two main **entrances** to the museum: the Puerta de Goya, which has an upper and a lower entrance opposite the *Hotel Ritz* on c/Felipe IV, and the Puerta de Murillo on Plaza de Murillo, in front of the Botanical Gardens, which often has shorter queues. **Floor plans** are available at each entrance and if you want more background on the key paintings there are audio guides (€3) or a good quick-visit guide (€9.90) in the bookshop.

▲ VELÁZQUEZ STATUE OUTSIDE THE PRADO

The comprehensive coverage of **Spanish paintings** begins on the ground floor with some striking twelfth-century Romanesque frescoes. Beyond and continuing upstairs is a stunning anthology that includes just about every significant

Spanish painter from the adopted Cretan-born artist El Greco (Domenikos Theotocopulos), who worked in Toledo in the 1570s, to Francisco de Goya, the outstanding painter of eighteenth-century Bourbon Spain. Don't miss the breathtaking collection of work by Diego Velázquez, including his masterpiece, *Las Meninas*, on the first floor (see box on p.90).

Nor would any visit be complete without seeing Goya's deeply evocative works, *Dos de Mayo* and *Tres de Mayo*, and his disturbing series of murals known as the *Pinturas Negras* (*Black Paintings*) with their mix of witches, fights to the death and child-eating gods.

The **Italian paintings** include the most complete collection by painters from the Venice school in any single museum, among them Titian's magnificent equestrian poratrait, *Emperor Carlos V at Mühlberg*. There are major works by Raphael and epic masterpieces from Tintoretto, Veronese, and Caravaggio too.

The early **Flemish works** are even more impressive and contain one of Hieronymus Bosch's greatest triptychs, the hallucinogenic *Garden of Earthly Delights*. Look out, too, for the works of Pieter Brueghel the Elder, whose *Triumph of Death* must be one of the most frightening canvases ever painted, Rogier van der Weyden's magnificent *Descent from the Cross*, and the extensive Rubens collection.

German, French and British painting is less well represented but still worth seeking out – especially the pieces by Dürer and Poussin –

while downstairs in the basement is a glittering display of the **jewels** that belonged to the Grand Dauphin Louis, son of Louis XIV and father of Felipe V, Spain's first Bourbon king.

Museo Thyssen-Bornemisza

ⓦwww.museothyssen.org. Tues–Sun 10am–7pm; occasionally till 10pm July & Aug, but check beforehand. €6 for permanent collection, €3 for temporary exhibitions, combined ticket €7. This fabulous private collection, assembled by Baron Heinrich Thyssen-Bornemisza, his son Hans Heinrich and his wife Carmen, was first displayed here in 1993 and contains pieces by almost every major Western artist since the fourteenth century.

The **new extension**, built on the site of an adjoining mansion and cleverly integrated into the original format of the museum, houses Carmen's collection, which is particularly strong on nineteenth-century landscape, North American, Impressionist and Post-Impressionist work.

The museum **shop** stocks a range of informative books on the leading artists, while audio guides (€3) are available at the desk in the main hall.

To follow the collection chronologically, begin on the **second floor** with pre-

▲ THE THYSSEN'S NEW EXTENSION

Renaissance work from the fourteenth century. This is followed by a wonderful array of Renaissance portraits by, amongst others, Ghirlandaio, Raphael and Holbein, including the latter's commanding *Henry VIII*. Beyond are some equally impressive pieces by Titian, Tintoretto, El Greco, Caravaggio and Canaletto, while a superb collection of landscapes and some soothing Impressionist works by Pissarro, Monet, Renoir, Degas and Sisley are housed in the new galleries.

The **first floor** continues with an evocative series of white marble sculptures by Rodin and an outstanding selection of work by Gauguin and

▼ *THE WITCHES' SABBATH*, GOYA, THE PRADO

▲ LIFTS OUTSIDE REINA SOFÍA

apocalyptic *Metropolis* by George Grosz.

The **ground floor** covers the period from the beginning of the twentieth century through to around 1970. Outstanding Cubist work from Picasso, Braque and Mondrian is to be found within the "experimental avant-garde" section. Look out too for some marvellous pieces by Miró, Pollock and Chagall. Surrealism is, not surprisingly, repre-sented by Dalí, while the final galleries include some eye-catching work by Bacon, Lichtenstein and Freud.

the Post-Impressionists. There's excellent coverage, too, of the vivid Expressionist work of Kandinsky, Nolde and Kirchner.

Beyond, the displays include a comprehensive round of seventeenth-century Dutch painting of various genres and some excellent nineteenth-cen-tury American landscapes. There are strong contributions from Van Gogh – most notably one of his last and most gorgeous works, *Les Vessenots* – and more from the Expressionists, including the

Centro de Arte Reina Sofía

🌐museoreinasofia.mcu.es. Mon & Wed–Sat 10am–9pm, Sun 10am–2.30pm. €3, free Sat after 2.30pm & all day Sun and for under-18s and over-65s. The other essential stop on the Madrid art circuit is the Centro de Arte Reina Sofía, an immense exhibition space providing a permanent home for the Spanish collection of modern and contemporary art.

The museum, a vast former hospital, has just undergone a 79

Guernica

Superbly displayed and no longer protected by bullet-proof glass and steel gird-ers, Picasso's *Guernica* is a monumental icon of twentieth-century Spanish art and politics which, despite its familiarity, still has the ability to shock. Picasso painted it in response to the bombing of the Basque town of Gernika in April 1937 by the German Luftwaffe, acting in concert with Franco, during the Spanish Civil War. In the preliminary studies, displayed around the room, you can see how he developed its symbols – the dying horse, the woman mourning, the bull and so on – and then return to the painting to marvel at how he made it all work. Picasso determined that the work be "loaned" to the Museum of Modern Art in New York while Franco remained in power, meaning that the artist never lived to see it displayed in his home country – it only returned to Spain in 1981, eight years after Picasso's death and six after the demise of Franco.

million-euro extension programme that has added a massive state-of-the-art metal and
glass triangular-shaped wing
behind the main block, allowing
more space for temporary exhibitions.

An informative **guide** is available from the shop (€9.90) and
there are audio guides (€3) at
the entrance.

The permanent collection
begins on the **second floor**
with a section examining the
origins of modern Spanish art,
largely through the two artistic
nuclei that developed in
Catalunya and the Basque
Country at the end of the nineteenth century.

Midway round the collection
is the Reina Sofía's main draw –
Picasso's *Guernica* (see box), a
controversial piece that has
always evoked strong reactions.
Strong sections on Cubism
and the Paris School follow, in
the first of which Picasso is
again well represented. Dalí and
Miró make heavyweight contributions too, while an impressive
collection of Spanish sculpture is
to be found in the final rooms.

The collection continues on
the **fourth floor**, although here
it's no match for the attractions
of the previous exhibits. This
section covers Spain's postwar
years up to the present day and
includes Spanish and interna-

▲ DALÍ'S *DREAM CAUSED BY THE FLIGHT OF A BEE . . .*, REINA SOFÍA

tional examples of abstract and avant-garde movements such as Pop Art, Constructivism and Minimalism, one of the highlights being Francis Bacon's *Figura Tumbada* (*Reclining Figure*).

There are also some striking pieces by the Basque abstract sculptor, Chillida, and Catalan Surrealist painter Tàpies.

Shops

Objectos de Arte Toledano

Paseo del Prado 10. Mon–Sat 9.30am–8pm. All-purpose souvenir shop stocking "typical Spanish"-style goods including fans, Lladró porcelain, T-shirts and tacky flamenco accessories.

Piel del Toro

Paseo del Prado 42. Mon–Fri 10am–8.30pm, Sat & Sun 11am–8pm. A colourful range of T-shirts, sweatshirts and baseball caps, all emblazoned with the emblem of a bull. Despite the clichéd image they make good, lightweight presents.

Cafés

Café el Botánico

C/Ruiz de Alarcón 27. Daily 8.30am–midnight. An ideal place for a morning coffee or an afternoon drink after a Prado visit, this place serves good beer and a small selection of delicious canapés and tapas.

Restaurants

Ancha

C/Zorrilla 7 ☎914 298 186. 1.30–4pm & 9pm–midnight. Closed Sun & hols. Highly regarded and rather expensive restaurant, popular with politicians from the nearby parliament. Mahogany-panelled decor and imaginative variations on traditional Castilian dishes are on offer. The pricey but good-quality lunchtime *menú* is €26.50.

Edelweiss

C/Jovellanos 7 ☎915 323 383. 1–4pm & 8pm–midnight, closed Sun eve. Quality German restaurant with good service, an authentic array of central European specialities and large portions. Expect to pay around €35 a head, although a more economical option is the €17.65 lunchtime menu.

Mesón la Pilarica

Paseo del Prado 40. Daily 9am–11pm. One of the nearest decent places to the Prado, this is a good spot to sample *jamón serrano* and other classic tapas. It does a basic lunchtime menu for €8 or a more elaborate offering for €12.50.

Taj

C/Marqués de Cubas 6 ☎915 315 059. Daily 1–4pm & 8.30pm–midnight. Friendly service and quality Indian food in this traditional curry house – go for some of the good starters and a tasty chicken tikka masala. Prices are reasonable too at around €25–30 a head.

La Tapería del Prado

Plaza Platerías de Martínez 1 ☎914 294 094. Daily 7.30am–12.30am. Modern and slightly pricey bar serving up an inventive range of tapas and *raciones* plus a decent set lunch at around €9.50. Portions are on the small side though.

Tapas bars

El Brilliante

Glorieta del Emperador Carlos V 8. Daily 6.30am–12.30am. Popular, down-to-earth bar, with long opening hours and a wide range of tapas and sandwiches making it a great place for a quick snack in between museum visits.

Cervecería Cervantes

Plaza de Jesús 7. Mon–Sat noon–12.30am, Sun noon–4pm. Great beer and fresh seafood tapas in this busy kitchen-like bar. The *gambas* (prawns) go down a treat with a cool class of the beer, while the *tosta de gambas* (a sort of prawn toast) is a must.

La Fábrica

Plaza de Jesús 2. Mon–Thurs & Sun 11am–1am, Fri & Sat 11am–2am. Bustling, friendly bar serving a delicious range of canapés, chilled beer and good vermouth. There's seating at the back for tapas if you want to linger for longer.

La Platería

C/Moratín 49. Mon–Fri 7.30am–1am, Sat & Sun 9.30–1am. This bar has an enormously popular summer *terraza* and a good selection of tasty and reasonably priced tapas available at any time of the day. Service can be a little brusque though.

La Taberna de Dolores

Plaza de Jesús 4. Daily 11am–midnight. Splendid canapés at this popular standing-room-only tiled bar. Decorated with beer bottles from around the world, the beer is really good and the food specialities include Roquefort and anchovy, and smoked-salmon canapés.

Discobares and clubs

Ananda

Avda Ciudad de Barcelona. June to mid-Sept; daily 10pm till late. A massive summer multi-*terraza* that attracts a glamorous clientele. Get here early to grab one of the comfy sofas and, if you don't fancy people-watching, there are concerts, talent contests and exhibitions to keep you entertained.

Kapital

C/Atocha 125. Open Thurs–Sun midnight–6am. From €12. Seven-floor macroclub catering for practically every taste with three dance floors, lasers, go-go dancers, a cinema and a top-floor *terraza*. Varied musical menu of disco, merengue, salsa, *sevillanas* and even some karaoke, plus its own "after hours" session from noon on Sundays.

The Retiro and around

The area around the Paseo del Prado is the site of two of the city's most beautiful green spaces: the peaceful Jardines Botánicos and the Parque del Retiro, a delightful mix of formal gardens and wider open spaces. The district is also home to a host of lesser-known sights, from the impressively renovated Estación de Atocha to a number of small museums, including the fascinating Real Fábrica de Tapices (Royal Tapestry Workshop). It isn't an area renowned for its bars, restaurants and nightlife, but there are still enough decent places for a drink or lunchtime pitstop.

Parque del Retiro

The origins of the wonderful Parque del Retiro (Retiro Park) go back to the early seventeenth century when Felipe IV produced a plan for a new palace and French-style gardens, the Buen Retiro. Of the buildings, only the ballroom (Casón del Buen Retiro) and the Hall of Realms (Museo del Ejército) remain.

The park itself has been public property for over a hundred years. Its 330-acre expanse offers the chance to jog, rollerblade, cycle, picnic, row on the lake (you can rent boats by the Monumento a Alfonso XII), have your fortune told, and – above all – promenade. The busiest day is Sunday, when half of Madrid turns out for the *paseo* and there are plenty of stalls and cafés for snack breaks.

Promenading aside, there's almost always something going on in the park, including concerts in the Quiosco de Música, performances by groups of South American musicians by the lake and, on summer weekends, puppet shows by the Puerta de Alcalá entrance.

Travelling **art exhibitions** are frequently housed in the graceful

▼ ROWING ON THE RETIRO'S LAKE

Palacio de Velázquez (May–Sept Mon & Wed–Sat 11am–8pm, Sun 11am–4pm; Oct–April Mon & Wed–Sat 10am–6pm, Sun 10am–4pm; free), the splendid Palacio de Cristal (same hours; ☎915 746 614 for information; free) and Casa de Vacas (daily 10.30am–2.30pm & 4–8pm; closed Aug; free). Look out too for the **Ángel Caído** (Fallen Angel), supposedly the world's only public statue to Lucifer, in the south of the park, and the magnificently ostentatious statue to Alfonso XII by the lake.

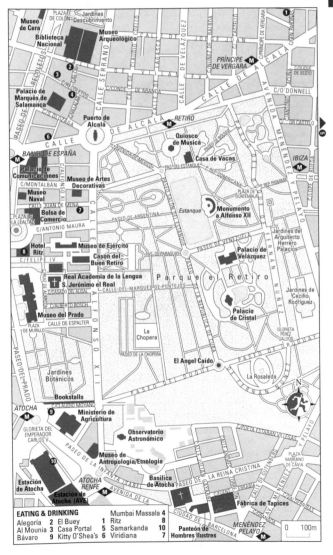

EATING & DRINKING

Alegoría	2	El Buey	1
Al Mounia	3	Casa Portal	5
Bávaro	9	Kitty O'Shea's	6

Mumbai Massala	4		
Ritz	8		
Samarkanda	10		
Viridiana	7		
Panteón de Hombres Ilustres			

0   100m

Puerta de Alcalá

The Puerta de Alcalá is one of Madrid's most emblematic landmarks. Built in Neoclassical style in 1769 by Francesco Sabatini to commemorate Carlos III's first twenty years on the throne, it was the biggest city gate in Europe at the time. Once on the site of the city's easternmost boundary, it's now marooned on a small island on the traffic-filled Plaza de la Independencia.

▲ THE BOTANICAL GARDENS

Jardines Botánicos

Plaza Murillo 2. Daily 10am–dusk. €2. The delightful and shaded Jardines Botánicos (Botanical Gardens) were opened in 1781 by Carlos III. The king's aim was to collect and grow species from all over his Spanish Empire, develop a research centre, and supply medicinal herbs and plants to Madrid's hospitals. However, the gardens were abandoned after the Peninsular War and, although they were renovated later in the nineteenth century and a zoo installed, they soon fell into disrepair once again. They were eventually restored in the 1980s, using the original eighteenth-century plans and are now home to some 30,000 species from around the globe. The collection of flora is fascinating for any amateur botanist and don't miss the hothouse with its tropical plants and amazing cacti.

Museo de Artes Decorativas

C/Montalbán 12 ⓦmnartesdecorativas .mcu.es. Tues–Sat 9.30am–3pm, Sun 10am–3pm. €2.40, free on Sun. The national collection of decorative arts is housed in a suitably aristocratic nineteenth-century mansion. The highlight is its collection of *azulejos* (tiles) and other ceramics with a magnificent eighteenth-century tiled Valencian kitchen on the top floor. The rest of the exhibits include an interesting but unspectacular collection of furniture, a series of reconstructed rooms and *objets d'art* from all over Spain.

Museo del Ejército

C/Méndez Núñez 1 ⓦwww.mde.es /mde/cultura/patrim/museo1.htm. Tues–Sun 10am–2pm. €0.60, free on Sat. A gloomily eccentric time-warp of a collection, the Museo del Ejército (Army Museum) is full of chaotically displayed military memorabilia from the Middle Ages onwards. Seemingly unaware of the changes over the past three decades, it preserves a distinctly pro-Franco stance. The motley but fascinating collection includes the tent used by Carlos I on a Tunisian campaign in

1535, a piece of the shirt worn by Pizarro when he was assassinated, a death mask of Napoleon and a room celebrating the exploits of the División Azul, the Spanish fascist volunteers who fought with the Germans in World War II.

Note that the museum is in the process of moving to the Alcázar in Toledo (see p.143), so displays are being gradually transferred.

▲ CERAMICS IN MUSEO DE ARTES DECORATIVAS

Museo Naval

Paseo del Prado 5 ⓦwww.museonaval-madrid.com. Tues–Sun 10am–2pm; closed Aug and public holidays. Free.
As you might expect, the Naval Museum is strong on models, charts and navigational aids relating to Spanish voyages of discovery. Exhibits include the first map to show the New World, drawn in 1500; cannons from the Spanish Armada; part of Cortés' standard used during the conquest of Mexico; and some giant, late seventeenth-century globes. The room dedicated to the *Nao San Diego*, which was sunk during a conflict with the Dutch off the Philippines in 1600, contains fascinating items recovered during the salvage operation in the early 1990s.

San Jerónimo el Real

C/Ruiz de Alarcón 19. Mon–Sat 10am–1pm & 5–8.30pm, Sun 9.30am–2.30pm & 5.30–8.30pm.
Madrid's high-society church was built on the site of a monastery founded in the early sixteenth century by the Catholic monarchs, Fernando and Isabel. An important destination for religious processions, it also became the venue for the swearing-in of the heirs to the throne and setting for many royal marriages and coronations (including the current king, Juan Carlos, in 1975). Despite significant remodelling and two Gothic towers added in the mid-nineteenth century, the old form of the church is still clearly visible; but the seventeenth-century cloisters have fallen victim to the controversial Prado extension plan (see p.91).

Real Academia Española de la Lengua

C/Ruiz de Alarcón 17. Fronted by a suitably imposing Neoclassical portico, the Royal Language Academy was established in 1714 by Felipe V to "cultivate and establish the purity and elegance of the Castilian language". Its job nowadays is to make sure that Spanish is not corrupted by foreign or otherwise unsuitable words and the academy's results are entrusted to their official dictionary – a work that bears virtually no relation to the Spanish spoken on the streets.

Plaza de la Lealtad

This aristocratic semicircular plaza contains the **Monumento a los Caídos por España** (Monument to Spain's Fallen).

▲ PLAZA DE LA LEALTAD

Originally a memorial to the Madrileños who died in the 1808 anti-French rebellion (the urn at the base contains the ashes of those killed), it was later changed to commemorate all those who have died fighting for Spain, and an eternal flame now burns here. On one side of the plaza stands the opulent *Ritz Hotel* (see pp.105 & 164), work of Charles Mewès, architect of the *Ritz* hotels in Paris and London. Opposite is the elegant colonnaded Bolsa de Comercio (Spain's stock exchange).

Estación de Atocha

The impressive Estación de Atocha is now sadly infamous as the scene of the horrific train bombings that killed 191 people and injured close to 2000 in March 2004. The bomb attacks took place in the modern section that services the local commuter lines and there are few Madrileños who do not pass through without paying silent respect to the victims.

The **old station** alongside was revamped in 1992 and is a glorious 1880s glasshouse, resembling a tropical garden. It's a wonderful sight from the walkways above, as a constant spray of water rains down on the jungle of vegetation. On the platforms beyond sit the gleaming high-speed AVE trains.

Ministry of Agriculture

Glorieta del Emperador Carlos V.
Overblown and hard to miss, the Ministry of Agriculture was designed in 1893 to epic proportions. Its exterior features decorative tile work and monumental caryatids representing Industry and Agriculture, while the whole thing is crowned with a striking figure of Glory, flanked by winged horses.

Museo Nacional de Antropología/Etnología

C/Alfonso XII 68 ⓜmnantropologia
.mcu.es. Tues–Sat 10am–7.30pm, Sun
10am–2pm. €2.40, free Sat after
2.30pm & Sun. The National Anthropology and Ethnography Museum was founded by the eccentric Dr Pedro González Velasco to house his private collection. The generally unimaginative displays give an overview of different cultures, in particular those linked to Spanish history. The most interesting exhibits are in a side room on the ground floor – a macabre collection of deformed skulls, a Guanche mummy (the original inhabitants of the Canary

▲ AVE HIGH-SPEED TRAINS, ATOCHA STATION

Islands), shrivelled embryos and the skeleton of a circus giant (2.35m tall) from whom Velasco had agreed to buy the skeleton after his death – payment in advance of course.

Real Fábrica de Tapices

C/Fuentarrabía 2 ⓦwww.realfatapices.com. Mon–Fri 10am–2pm; closed Aug. €3; tours every half an hour (guides usually speak English). The Royal Tapestry Workshop makes for a fascinating visit. Founded in 1721 and moved to its present site in the nineteenth century, the factory uses processes and machines unchanged for hundreds of years, including original eighteenth-century vertical looms. The workers, now numbering around 75 compared to four hundred half a century ago, can be seen coolly looping handfuls of bobbins around myriad strings, sewing up worn-out masterpieces with exactly matching silk, and weaving together different shades for a new tapestry. With progress being painfully slow – one worker produces a square metre of tapestry every three and a half months – the astronomical prices soon seems easily understandable. One of the giant sixteenth-century Flemish tapestries on display took more than two generations to complete.

Panteón de Hombres Ilustres

C/Julián Gayarre 3 ⓦwww.patrimonionacional.es. April–Sept Mon–Sat 9am–7pm, Sun 9am–4pm; Oct–March Mon–Sat 9.30am–6pm, Sun 9am–3pm. Free. Built adjacent to the Real Basílica de Atocha, this late eighteenth-century Byzantine-style building was meant to serve as a mausoleum for the most important figures in Madrid's history. The full extent of the plans was never realised and many of the bodies have since been removed. There are, however, some impressively

▼ REAL FÁBRICA DE TAPICES

elaborate marble tombs commemorating nineteenth-century politicians, many of whom were assassinated during this turbulent period in the city's history.

Shops

Cuesta Moyano

Cuesta de Claudio Moyano. The hilly street of Cuesta Moyano is lined with little wooden kiosks selling just about every book you could think of, from second-hand copies of Captain Marvel to Cervantes or Jackie Collins. Apart from the books, there's always something of interest, such as old prints of Madrid and relics from the Franco era. Although the street's at its busiest on Sundays, some of the stalls are open every day.

and models of ships. Dinner costs around €30.

Al Mounia

C/Recoletos 5 ☎914 350 828. Tues–Sat 1.30–3.30pm & 9pm–midnight. Closed Aug. Moroccan cooking at its best in the most established Arabic restaurant in town, offering an atmospheric and romantic setting with impeccable service. The couscous and desserts are a must, but prices are high with main courses costing around €18.

El Buey

C/General Pardiñas 10 ☎914 314 492. Mon–Sat 1–4pm & 9pm–midnight, Sun 1–4pm. Excellent Argentine-style meat dishes in this cramped little restaurant near the Retiro. Prices – €30–35 per person – are pretty reasonable considering the high quality.

▲ BOOKSTALLS ON CUESTA MOYANO

Restaurants

Alegoría/Alquimia

C/Villanueva 2 (entrance on C/Cid) ☎915 772 785. Daily 9pm–5am. Modelled on an English gentleman's club, this restaurant, bar and disco rolled into one comes complete with a library

Casa Portal

C/Dr Castelo 26 ☎915 742 026. Tues–Sat 1.30–4pm & 8.30–11.30pm. Closed hols & Aug. Superlative Asturian cooking – go for the *fabada* (beans, chorizo and black pudding stew) or *besugo* (bream), washed down with some cider. The shellfish is excellent too. Around €35 per person.

Mumbai Massala

C/Recoletos 14 ☎914 357 194,
ⓦwww.mumbaimassala.com. Daily
1.30–3.30pm & 9–11.30pm. Palatial
decor in this upmarket Indian
restaurant serving a wide range
of very good, but very expensive, curries – all the usual
favourites are available. Evening
prices are in the region of €37
a head, but a better alternative is
the lunchtime menu for just
€12.

Samarkanda

Estación de Atocha ☎915 309 746.
Daily 1.30–4pm & 9pm–midnight.
Light years away from the
typical fare at your average
railway station, this colonial-
style restaurant, perched
alongside the tropical garden,
serves excellent and imaginative
dishes such as ostrich steak in
sweet and sour sauce. It can,
however, get unbearably hot in
summer. Main courses cost
€12–16 or there's also a small
café for a drink and a snack.

Viridiana

C/Juan de Mena 14 ☎915 234 478 or
915 311 039. Mon–Sat 1.30–4pm &
9pm–midnight. Closed Easter & Aug.
Bizarre temple of Madrid *nueva
cocina* (new cuisine), decorated
with photos from Luis Buñuel's
film of the same name and
offering mouthwatering cre-
ations from a constantly changing menu, plus a superb selection of wines. The bill is likely
to come to around €70 a head
but it's an unforgettable experience.

Bars

Bávaro

Cuesta Claudio Moyano. Daily
noon–3am. Perched on a little
island of grass and with views
towards Atocha, this *terraza*
makes a great stop at any time
of the day or night.

Kitty O'Shea's

C/Alcalá 59. Mon–Thurs & Sun
11am–2am, Fri & Sat 11am–3am.
Spacious Irish bar offering the
usual mixture of Irish beers and
TV sports, plus plenty of very
reasonable pub-style food.

The Ritz

Plaza de la Lealtad 5. Breakfast
7.30–11am, tea 4.30–7.30pm, drinks
and tapas 7.30pm–1am. For a
glimpse of how the other half
live, try afternoon English-style
tea or early-evening cocktails in
the luxurious surroundings of
the *Ritz*.

Gran Vía, Chueca and Malasaña

The Gran Vía, one of Madrid's main thoroughfares, effectively divides the old city to the south from the newer parts in the north. Permanently heaving with traffic, shoppers and sightseers, it's the commercial heart of the city, and quite a monument in its own right, with its turn-of-the-twentieth-century, palace-like banks and offices, and the huge hand-painted posters of its cinemas. North of here, and bursting with bars, restaurants and nightlife, are two of the city's most characterful barrios: Chueca, focal point of Madrid's gay scene, and neighbouring Malasaña, former centre of the *Movida Madrileña*, the happening scene of the late 1970s and early 1980s, and still a somewhat alternative area, focusing on lively Plaza Dos de Mayo. As well as the bustling atmosphere, a couple of museums and a number of beautiful churches in the area provide even more reasons for a visit.

Gran Vía

The Gran Vía (Great Way) was built in three stages over nearly half a century and became a symbol of Spain's arrival in the twentieth century. Financed on the back of an economic boom experienced as a result of the country's neutrality in World War I, the Gran Vía is a showcase for a whole gamut of architectural styles, from Modernist and Art Deco to Neo-Rococo and Rationalist.

The finest section is the earliest, constructed between 1910 and 1924 and stretching from c/Alcalá to the Telefónica skyscraper. Particularly noteworthy are the **Edificio Metrópolis** (1905–1911), complete with cylindrical facade, white stone sculptures, zinc-tiled roof and gold garlands, and the nearby **Grassy** building (1916–17), which is equally overblown.

Further along, the vast 81-metre-high slab of the **Telefónica** building, with its

▼ GRAN VÍA

plain sand-coloured facade, was Spain's first skyscraper. During the Civil War, the building was used as a reference point by Franco's forces to bomb the Gran Vía.

The stretch down to Plaza de Callao is dominated by shops, cafés and cinemas with their massive hand-painted posters, while the plaza itself is now the gateway to the shoppers' paradise of c/Preciados. On the corner is the classic Art Deco **Capitol** building (1930–33), its curved facade embellished with lurid neon signs.

Cast your eyes skywards on the final stretch downhill towards Plaza de España to catch site of an assortment of statues and decorations that top many of the buildings on this more modern section.

The area has been rejuvenated in recent years and from Plaza de Chueca east to Paseo de Recoletos you'll find some of the city's most enticing streets. Offbeat restaurants, small private art galleries and unusual corner shops are here in abundance. C/Almirante has some of the city's most fashionable clothes shops and c/Augusto Figueroa is the place to go if you're looking for shoes.

La Casa de las Siete Chimeneas

Plaza del Rey 1. The sixteenth-century House of Seven Chimneys is allegedly haunted by an illegitimate daughter of Felipe II who disappeared in mysterious circumstances. The building – which now houses offices belonging to the

▲ PLAZA DE CHUECA

Plaza de Chueca

The smaller streets immediately north of Gran Vía are home to all manner of vice-related activities and are notorious for petty crime. However, in Plaza de Chueca and the barrio around it there's a strong neighbourhood feel, with kids and grannies on the streets during the day, and a lively gay scene at night.

Ministry of Culture – has been heavily restored, but is still rec-ognizable as the work of El Escorial architects, Juan Bautista de Toledo and Juan de Herrera, with its red-brick and slate turret. Charles I of England stayed here when he came to Madrid to press his unsuccessful suit for marriage to the Infanta María.

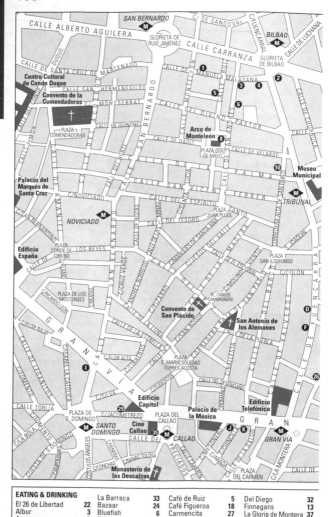

EATING & DRINKING		La Barraca	33	Café de Ruiz	5	Del Diego	32
El 26 de Libertad	22	Bazaar	24	Café Figueroa	18	Finnegans	13
Albur	3	Bluefish	6	Carmencita	27	La Gloria de Montera	37
Annapurna	7	El Bocaito	30	Chicote	36	Gula Gula	38
Azul Profundo	17	Café Acuarela	15	El Comunista		La Isla del Tesoro	4
Bar Plaza Dos de Mayo	8	Café Comercial	2	(Tienda de Vinos)	19	Kingston's	16

Las Salesas Reales

Plaza de Las Salesas. 9am–1.30pm &
6–9pm. The convent complex of
Las Salesas Reales was founded
in 1747 by Barbara of Bragança,
Portuguese wife of Fernando VI.
Santa Barbara church, with its
impressive Baroque facade decorated with marble statues, is set
behind a fine forecourt containing a rose garden, palm trees and
magnolias. Inside, there's a
grotto-like chapel, impressive
frescoes and stained-glass windows, an extravagant pulpit and
striking green marble altar dec-

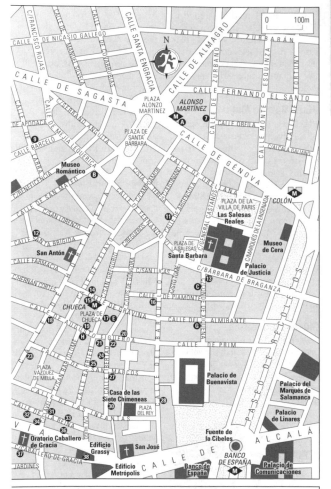

				SHOPS		Casa Postal	**E**
Liquid	**28**	Pachá	**9**	Taberna		Pasajes	**A**
Momo	**20**	Ribeiro do Miño	**12**	Angel Sierra **14**	Ararat **G**	Bazar Mila	**F**
La Musa	**1**	Salvador	**25**	La Tasca	Bazar Mila **J**	Glam	
Oba-Oba	**29**	Santander	**21**	Suprema	**11**	Caligae **H**	Mercado Fuencarral **D**
Ohm/Bash Line/		Stop Madrid	**26**	Tupperware **10**	Camper **I**	Reserva y Cata **C**
Weekend	**35**	Taberna de Sarmiento **23**	XXX Café	**31**	Casa del Libro **K**	Tienda Olivarero **B**

oration. The elaborate tomb of Fernando VI lies in the main church, as does that of the military hero General O'Donnell, while Barbara herself has been relegated to a side chapel.

The convent behind the church now houses the Palacio de Justicia, the city's Law Courts, facing the elegant Plaza de la Villa de París.

Sociedad de Autores

C/Fernando VI 4. Home to the Society of Authors, this is the most significant Modernista building in Madrid. Designed in 1902 by the Catalan architect José Grasés Riera, its facade features a dripping decoration of flowers, faces and balconies giving the appearance of a melting candle.

Plaza Dos de Mayo

Plaza Dos de Mayo is the centre of the lively Malasaña bar scene with customers spilling on to the streets that converge on the square. The plaza commemorates the rebellion against occupying French troops in 1808, while the neighborhood gets its name from a young seamstress, Manuela Malasaña, who became one of the rebellion's heroines. Legend has it that she was executed for carrying a weapon (her scissors) after she was searched by the occupiers on her way home from work.

Museo Romántico

C/San Mateo 13 ⓦmuseoromantico .mcu.es. Closed for refurbishment until 2005, though usually open Tues–Sat 9am–3pm, Sun & hols 10am–2pm; closed Aug. €2.40, free on Sun. The

▼ FACADE OF MUSEO MUNICIPAL

Museo Romántico aims to show the lifestyles and ideas of the late-Romantic era through the re-creation of a typical period residence (the building itself dates back to the late eighteenth century). It's a pretty successful attempt, with its musty atmosphere, creaking floorboards, cracking walls crowded with canvases, and rooms overflowing with kitsch memorabilia and furniture.

Museo Municipal

C/Fuencarral 78 ⓦwww.munimadrid.es /museomunicipal. Currently closed for refurbishment (an interesting selection of key exhibits is on show in the chapel), though usually open Tues–Fri 9.30am–8pm, Sat & Sun 10am–2pm; Aug: Tues–Sun 10am–2pm. Free. The Museo Municipal is housed in the former city almshouse, remodelled in the early eighteenth century by Pedro de Ribera, who gave it a fantastically decorated Baroque doorway placed on an otherwise plain red-brick facade.

Inside is a chronological collection of paintings, photos, models, sculptures and porcelain, all relating to the history and urban development of Madrid since 1561 (the date it was designated imperial capital by Felipe II) through to the twentieth century. The eighteenth-century **chapel** on the ground floor survives from the time de Ribera remodelled the building and contains a dramatic canvas, *San Fernando ante la Virgen*, above the altar.

San Antonio de los Alemanes

Corredera de San Pablo 16. Daily 9am–1pm & 6–8pm. Free. One of the city's hidden treasures, this little church was designed in 1624 by the Jesuit architect, Pedro Sánchez, and Juan Gómez de Mora. The elliptical interior is lined with dizzying floor-to-ceiling pastel-coloured frescoes by Neapolitan artist Luca Giordano which depict scenes from the life of St Anthony.

▲ FRESCOES IN SAN ANTONIO

Shops

Ararat

C/Almirante 10 & 11. Mon–Sat 11am–2pm & 5–8.30pm. Two shops with Spanish and foreign designers for men, women and children at reasonably modest prices. The women's shop at no. 10 specializes in more formal wear, while no. 11 goes for a younger, more modern look.

Bazar Mila

Gran Vía 33. Mon–Sat 9.30am–8.30pm. Decent toy shop that is just the place to get your Spanish set of Monopoly or your plastic models of Real and Atlético players.

Caligae

C/Augusto Figueroa 27. Mon–Fri 10am–2pm & 5–8pm, Sat 10.30am–2pm & 5–8pm. One of a string of shoe shops located on this busy Chueca street selling discounted designer footwear. If you're on the lookout for some sandals, fashion trainers, party shoes or boots, then this is the place to come.

Camper

C/Gran Vía 54. Mon–Sat 10am–2pm & 5–8.30pm. Spain's best shoe-shop chain, selling practical and comfortable designs at modest prices, with the odd quirky fabric and unusual heel thrown in. There are lots of other branches around the city.

Casa del Libro

Gran Vía 29 and c/Maestro Victoria 3. Mon–Sat 9.30am–9.30pm. The Casa del Libro's Gran Vía branch is the city's biggest bookshop, with four floors covering just about everything, including a wide range of fiction in English and translations of classic Spanish works. The branch at Maestro Victoria has a good section of maps, guides and books about Madrid.

Casa Postal

C/Libertad 37. Mon–Fri 10am–2pm & 5–8.30pm, Sat 10.30am–2pm. Marvellous old-fashioned shop for lovers of nostalgia, packed with postcards, posters and other original mementos of the city.

Glam

C/Fuencarral 35. Mon–Fri 10am–3pm & 4–9pm, Sat 11am–9.30pm, Sun noon–3pm & 4–9pm. Club/street-style clothes that wouldn't look out of place in an Almodóvar film. Good-value shirts and tops too. There's a shoe shop with wacky trainers and trendy footwear next door.

▲ SHOP ON C/FUENCARRAL

Tienda Olivarero

C/Mejia Lequerica 1. Mon–Sat 10am–2pm & 5.30–7.30pm. This outlet for an olive-growers' co-operative has useful information sheets to help you buy the best olive oils.

Cafés

Café Acuarela

C/Gravina 10. Daily 3pm–3am, Fri & Sat till 4am. Very comfortable café, with over-the-top Baroque decor and great cocktails – the perfect place for a quiet drink. Popular with a mostly gay/lesbian crowd.

Mercado Fuencarral

C/Fuencarral 45. Mon–Sat 10am–10pm. Shopping mall catering for the young fashion-conscious crowd, filled with clubwear shops, record stores, jewellers, a café and even a tattoo parlour.

Pasajes

C/Genova 3. Mon–Fri 10am–2pm & 5–8pm, Sat 10am–2pm. Interesting bookshop, specializing in English and foreign-language titles, plus language-learning aids.

Reserva y Cata

C/Conde de Xiquena 13. Mon–Fri 11am– 2.30pm, Sat 11am–2.30pm. Well-informed staff at this friendly specialist shop will help you select from some of the best new wines in the Iberian peninsula. Branch at c/Ramiro II 7.

Café Comercial

Glorieta de Bilbao 7. Daily 8am–1am, Fri & Sat till 2am. A Madrileño institution and one of the city's most popular meeting points, this is a lovely traditional café full of mirrors, large tables and a cross section of Madrid society.

Café de Ruiz

C/Ruiz 11. Daily 3pm–2am. Classic old-fashioned Malasaña café and a great place to while away an afternoon. Discreet background music and good cakes are followed by cocktails in the evening.

Café Figueroa

C/Augusto Figueroa 17. Mon–Thurs 2.30pm–1am, Fri & Sat 2.30pm–2.30am, Sun 4pm–1am. Opened in the early 1980s, this is an established institution on the Madrileño gay scene, with regulars of all ages, a pool table upstairs and great parties during *Carnaval*.

XXX Café

Gran Vía 16, entrance on c/Clavel. Mon–Thurs & Sun 3.30pm–2am, Fri & Sat 3.30pm–3am. Chic, straight-friendly café/club with a mainly gay clientele. A good place to browse the paper during the day over some excellent carrot cake and coffee, it livens up at night, with cabaret and drag shows in the basement at weekends.

Restaurants

El 26 de Libertad

C/Libertad 26 ☎915 222 522. Mon 1–4pm, Tues–Thurs 1–4pm & 8pm–midnight, Fri & Sat 1–4pm & 9pm–midnight. Imaginative cuisine served up in an attentive but unfussy manner in this brightly decorated restaurant, popular with the Chueca locals. The good-value lunch *menú* is €9, evening main courses €8–15. The front bar serves some excellent tapas too.

Annapurna

C/Zurbano 5 ☎913 198 716. Mon–Fri 1.30–4pm & 9pm–midnight, Sat 9pm–midnight. One of the better Indian restaurants in Madrid, especially if you go for the tandoori dishes or *thali*. Elegant surroundings and attentive service too, all for around €30–35 per person.

Azul Profundo

Plaza Chueca 8 ☎915 322 564. Tues–Sat 1.30–3.30pm & 9pm–midnight. Closed first three weeks in Aug. Bright blue decor, superb creative cuisine and a welcoming atmosphere in this small restaurant that serves up an excellent *menú de degustación* at €30.

La Barraca

C/Reina 29 ☎915 327 154. Daily 1–4pm & 8.30pm–midnight. Step off the dingy street into this little piece of Valencia for some of the best paella in town. Service is attentive, the starters are excellent and there's a great lemon sorbet for dessert too. A three-course meal with wine costs around €35 a head.

Bazaar

C/Libertad 21 ☎915 233 905. Daily 1.15–4pm & 8.30–11.45pm. The quality fusion-style Mediterranean and Asian cuisine here has been a big hit on the Chueca scene. Lunchtime menu is just €8.30; evening meals under €20. No reservations so arrive early to avoid waiting.

Bluefish

C/ San Andrés 26 ☎914 486 765, ⊛www.bluefish.homestead.com/Home_e.html. Tues–Sat 8pm–1am, Sun 1–6pm. Imaginative food and a very good *menú* for €9 at this trendy restaurant-bar-cocktail joint. Other Asian-influenced dishes go for around €8, and they do a great Sunday brunch too, including a Bloody Mary.

▲ CARMENCITA

Carmencita

C/Libertad 16 ☎915 316 612. Mon–Fri 1–4pm & 9pm–midnight, Sat 9pm–midnight. Beautiful old restaurant dating back to 1850, with plenty of brass, marble tables, Valencian tiles – and a Basque-influenced chef. The lunch *menú* is a bargain at under €10 – the speciality is the *cocido*, served on Thursdays – while à la carte prices bump the bill up considerably.

El Comunista (Tienda de Vinos)

C/Augusto Figueroa 35 ☎915 217 012. Mon–Sat 1–4.30pm & 9.30–11.45pm, Sun 9.30–11.45pm. Closed mid-Aug to mid-Sept. Long-established, popular *comedor* that has changed little since it was given its unofficial (but always used) name as a student haunt under Franco. The *sopa de ajo* (garlic soup) is particularly recommended. Expect to pay between €4–8 for main courses.

La Gloria de Montera

C/Caballero de Gracia 10. Metro Gran Vía. Daily 1–4.30pm & 8.30–11.45pm. Sister restaurant to *La Finca de Susana* (see p.85) with the same successful formula. Excellent value *menú* at €8.30 with imaginative, well-presented dishes on offer in a cool and airy setting. No reservations.

Gula Gula

Gran Vía 1 ☎915 228 764. Mon–Thurs 1–4.30pm & 9pm–2am, Fri & Sat 1–4.30pm & 9pm–3am. Spacious salad-bar-type restaurant that does an eat-as-much-as-you-can self-service buffet for around €20, and has live shows featuring drag queens and dancers every night. Popular for "hen nights" as well as with the gay crowd.

La Isla del Tesoro

C/Manuela Malasaña 3 ☎915 931 440. Mon–Sat 1.30–4pm & 9pm–12.30am, Sun 9pm–12.30am. Tropical beach decor and cosmopolitan vegetarian food at this good-value place. Service is not always up to standard however. The constantly changing *menú del día* is €8.90.

Momo

C/Augusto Figueroa 41 ☎915 327 162. Daily 1–4pm & 9pm–midnight. A well-established feature on the Chueca scene, this is the place to go for a *menú del día* with a little bit extra. For €8.50 you get three courses, with some imaginative sauces, drinks and coffee. Unusually for Spain they also do a set dinner in the evening for €12. Very popular.

La Musa

C/Manuela Malasaña 18 ☎914 487 558. Daily 1.30–4.30pm & 8.30pm–midnight. It's easy to see why *La Musa* is such a firm favourite on the Malasaña scene. A variety of imaginative and tasty tapas, a strong wine list and chic decor are all part of the recipe for success. The set lunch is €9.

Ribeira do Miño

C/Santa Brígida 1 ☎915 219 854. Tues–Sun 1–4pm & 8pm–1am. Great-value *marisquería*, serving a seafood platter for two at only €24.50; go for the slightly more expensive Galician white wine, Albariño, to accompany it. Efficient and friendly service.

Salvador

C/Barbieri 12 ☎915 214 524. Mon–Sat 1.30–4pm & 9pm–midnight. Closed Aug. Bullfighting decor and traditional favourites such as *pollo al ajillo* (garlic chicken) and *arroz con leche* (rice pudding). Lunchtime menu €25.

La Tasca Suprema

C/Argensola 7 ☎913 080 347.

Mon–Sat 1.30–4pm. Closed Aug. Very popular, family-run local, only open at lunchtimes and worth booking ahead for. Perfect Castilian home cooking, including, on Monday and Thursday, *cocido*. Main courses cost between €10 and €15.

Tapas bars

Albur
C/Manuela Malasaña 15. Sun–Wed noon–midnight, Thurs–Sat noon–1.30am. Rustic decor and excellent food, although service can be a little slow. The *champiñones en salsa verde* (mushrooms in a coriander sauce) and the *patatas albur* (potatoes with herbs and spices) are worth sampling. Lunchtime menu is €9.

El Bocaito
C/Libertad 4–6. Mon–Fri 1–4pm & 8.30pm–midnight, Sat 8.30pm–midnight. Closed two weeks in Aug. Watch the staff prepare the food in the kitchen as you munch away on a variety of delicious tapas. Look out for the *Luisito* (chilli, squid, mayonnaise and a secret sauce all topped with a prawn), the hottest canapé you're ever likely to encounter.

Santander
C/Augusto Figueroa 25. Mon–Sat 10.45am–4pm & 7.30–11pm. Closed Aug. Down-to-earth bar, famous for its vast range of tapas, including *tortillas* and quiche lorraine, as well as a huge variety of fresh home-made canapés at very reasonable prices.

Stop Madrid
C/Hortaleza 11. Mon–Sat noon–4pm & 7pm–midnight. An old-time spit-and-sawdust bar, specializing in dishes from Extremadura accompanied by Belgian, Mexican and German beers. Tapas consist largely of *jamón* and *chorizo*, with the Canapé Stop of ham and tomato doused in olive oil well worth a try.

Taberna de Sarmiento
C/Hortaleza 28. Mon–Thurs noon–4pm & 8pm–midnight, Fri noon–4pm & 8pm–1am, Sat 8pm–1am. One of the new wave of tapas bars, specializing in artistically presented sit-down tapas. Try the spinach croquettes or, for the more adventurous, the scallop, prawn and mango salad. Don't miss the selection of canapés, especially the paté with caramelized onion. Excellent selection of wines too.

Bars

Chicote
Gran Vía 12. Mon–Sat 5pm–1.30am. The place to go to wallow in nostalgia. Opened in 1931 by Perico Chicote, ex-barman at the *Ritz*, and still full of Art Deco lines and pistachio-coloured booths. Sophia Loren, Frank Sinatra, Ava Gardner, Luis Buñuel, Orson Welles and the ubiquitous Hemingway have all passed through its doors.

Del Diego
C/Reina 12. Mon–Sat 9pm–3am. Closed Aug. A smart New York–style cocktail bar set up by a former *Chicote* waiter who personally mixes all the excellent cocktails in a friendly, unhurried atmosphere. The house special, vodka-based Del Diego, is the one to go for.

Finnegans
Plaza de Las Salesas 9. Daily 1pm–2am. Large Irish bar with several rooms, complete with bar fittings and wooden floors

brought over from the Emerald Isle. English-speaking staff and TV sports, plus a pub quiz on Monday nights.

Plaza Dos de Mayo

Plaza Dos de Mayo. Mon–Thurs & Sun 1pm–2am, Fri & Sat 1pm–3am. Old-style wood-and-tiles bar that gets packed at weekends and that opens up in the summer so you can watch the goings-on in the square.

Taberna Ángel Sierra

C/Gravina 11, on Plaza Chueca. Daily noon–1am. One of the great bars in Madrid, where everyone drinks *vermút* accompanied by free, exquisite pickled anchovy tapas. *Raciones* are also available, though they're pretty pricey.

Clubs and discobares

Kingston's

C/Barquillo 29. Tues–Sat 11.30pm–5.30am. €8. Relaxed discobar, with colourful ethnic designs. Music ranges from soul and funk to reggae and rap and, at the weekend, professional dancers get things going.

Liquid

C/Barquillo 8. Tues–Thurs & Sun 9pm–3am, Fri & Sat 9pm–3.30am. Smart and stylish gay bar, lined with video screens playing a selection of fashionable music to an equally fashionable clientele.

Oba-Oba

C/Jacometrezo 6. Mon–Sat 11pm–4am. €8. Long-established Latin club with a small dance floor and a fun atmosphere. It often has live Brazilian music accompanied by the obligatory *caipirinhas* and daiquiris.

Ohm/Bash Line/Weekend

Plaza Callao 4. Wed 11pm–6am, Thurs–Sat midnight–6am, Sun midnight–5am. €10. One of the major venues on the Madrid club scene. Ohm is the main techno-house session on Friday and Saturday nights and is very popular with the gay crowd; Bash Line is for those who need a midweek hip-hop and soul fix; and Weekend is the Sunday session for those who don't like Mondays.

Pachá

C/Barceló 11 ⓦwww.pacha-madrid.com/tarde.html. Thurs–Sat midnight–5am. €12 with drink. Once a theatre – and still very dramatic – this eternal survivor on the Madrid clubbing scene is exceptionally cool during the week, less so at weekends when out-of-towners take over. Good if you like techno and house.

▲ PACHÁ

Tupperware

C/Corredera Alta de San Pablo 26. Daily 9pm–3.30am. The place to go for the latest on the indie scene, with a mix of grunge and classics from the punk era.

Salamanca and the Paseo de la Castellana

Exclusive Barrio de Salamanca was developed in the second half of the nineteenth century as an upmarket residential zone under the patronage of the Marquis of Salamanca. Today it's still home to Madrid's smartest apartments and designer emporiums, while the streets are populated by the chic clothes and sunglasses brigade, decked out in Gucci and gold. Shopping apart, there's a scattering of sights here, including the pick of the city's smaller museums and Real Madrid's imposing Santiago Bernabéu stadium. Bordering Salamanca to the west is the multi-lane Paseo de la Castellana, peppered with corporate office blocks, where, in summer, the section between Plaza de Colón and the Glorieta Emilio Castelar transforms into "*La Costa Castellana*", littered with trendy *terrazas* that play host to the city's beautiful people.

Plaza de Colón

Overlooking a busy crossroads and dominating the square in which they stand are a neo-Gothic monument to Christopher Columbus (Cristóbal Colón), given as a wedding gift to Alfonso XII, and an enormous Spanish flag. Directly behind are the Jardínes del Descubrimiento (Discovery Gardens), a small park containing three huge stone blocks representing Columbus's three ships. Below the plaza, underneath a cascading wall of water, is the 1970s **Centro Cultural de la Villa** (Tues–Sat 10am–9pm, Sat & Sun 10am–2pm), a good place for film, theatre and occasional exhibitions.

▼ PLAZA DE COLÓN

Biblioteca Nacional and Museo del Libro

Paseo de Recoletos 20 Ⓦwww.bne.es. Tues–Sat 10am–9pm, Sun & hols 10am–2pm. Free. The National Library contains over three million

Salamaca and the Paseo de la Castellana PLACES

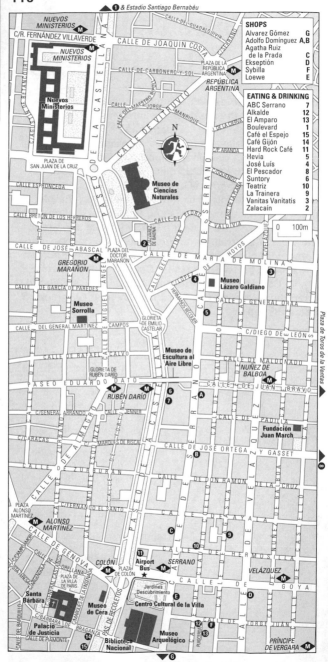

SHOPS

Alvarez Gómez	G
Adolfo Dominguez	A,B
Agatha Ruiz de la Prada	C
Ekseptión	D
Sybilla	F
Loewe	E

EATING & DRINKING

ABC Serrano	7
Alkalde	12
El Amparo	13
Boulevard	1
Café el Espejo	15
Café Gijón	14
Hard Rock Café	11
Hevia	5
José Luís	4
El Pescador	8
Suntory	6
Teatriz	10
La Trainera	9
Vanitas Vanitatis	3
Zalacaín	2

volumes, including every work published in Spain since 1716. The Museo del Libro (Book Museum) within displays a selection of the library's treasures, including Arab, Hebrew and Greek manuscripts, and has an interesting interactive exhibition on the development of written communication (in Spanish only).

Museo Arqueológico Nacional

C/Serrano 13 ⓦwww.man.es. Tues–Sat 9.30am–8.30pm, till 6.30pm in summer; Sun 9.30am–2.30pm. €3, free Sat after 2.30pm & all day Sun. The vast collections of the National Archeological Museum trace the cultural evolution of humankind. Most exhibits are from Spain and include striking **Celto-Iberian busts** known as *La Dama de Elche* and *La Dama de Baza*, as well as a wonderfully rich hoard of Visigothic treasures found at Toledo. Good coverage is also given to Roman, Egyptian, Greek and Islamic finds, but rooms are often closed for rearrangement.

In the gardens, a reconstruction of the prehistoric cave paintings of Altamira in Cantabria are the nearest you'll get to the real thing these days, since the caves themselves are now closed to the public.

Museo de Cera

Paseo de Recoletos 41 ⓦwww.museo-ceramadrid.com. Mon–Fri 10am–2.30pm & 4.30–8.30pm, Sat, Sun & hols 10am–8.30pm. €10. Over 450 different personalities – including a host of VIPs, heads of state and, of course, Real Madrid football stars – are displayed in this expensive and tacky museum, which is nevertheless popular with children. There's also a chamber of horrors and a film history of Spain (supplement charged).

Museo de Escultura al Aire Libre

Paseo de la Castellana 41 ⓦwww.munimadrid.es/museoairelibre. An innovative use of the space underneath the Juan Bravo flyover, the Open Air Sculpture Museum is made up of a haphazard collection, including work by Eduardo Chillida, Joan Miró and Julio González. The collection of cubes, walls, fountains and optical trickery appears to be most appreciated by the city's skateboard community.

Museo Sorolla

Paseo del General Martínez Campos 37 ⓦmuseosorolla.mcu.es. Tues–Sat 9.30am–3pm, Sun 10am–3pm. €2.40, free Sun. Part museum and part art gallery, this tribute to a single artist's life and work is one of Madrid's most underrated treasures. Situated in Joaquín Sorolla's former home – built in 1910 and donated to the nation by his widow in 1923 – it's a delightful oasis of peace and tranquillity, its cool and shady

▼ LA DAMA DE ELCHE

▲ MUSEO SOROLLA

Andalusian-style courtyard and gardens decked out with statues, fountains, assorted plants and fruit trees.

The ground floor has been kept largely intact, re-creating the authentic atmosphere of the artist's living and working areas. The upstairs rooms, originally the sleeping quarters, have been turned into a gallery, where sunlight, sea, intense colours, women and children dominate Sorolla's impressionistic paintings. On your way out, there's a small collection of his sketches and gouaches.

Museo Lázaro Galdiano

C/Serrano 122 ⓦwww.flg.es. Mon & Wed–Sun 10am–4.30pm. €4, free Wed. When businessman and publisher José Lázaro Galdiano died in 1947, he left his private collection – a vast treasure trove of paintings and *objets d'art* – to the state. Spread over the four floors of his former home, the collection contains jewellery, outstanding Spanish archeological pieces and some beautifully decorated thirteenth-century

Limoges enamels. There's also an excellent selection of **European paintings** with works by Bosch, Rembrandt, Reynolds and Constable, plus Spanish artists including Zurbarán, Velázquez, El Greco and Goya. Other exhibits include several clocks and watches, many of them once owned by Carlos V.

Museo de Ciencias Naturales

C/José Gutiérrez Abascal 2 ⓦwww.mncn.csic.es. Tues–Fri 10am–6pm, Sat 10am–8pm, Sun 10am–2.30pm. €2.40, free Sun. The Natural History Museum's displays are split between two buildings. One contains a fairly predictable collection of stuffed animals and audiovisual displays on the evolution of life on earth, the other is home to some rather dull fossil and geological exhibits.

Nuevos Ministerios and the Zona Azca

Paseo de la Castellana. Nuevos Ministerios is a vast monolithic complex of government buildings, initiated during the Second Republic but completed under Franco. The bleak facade is broken only by the entrance to some gardens which are open to the public. A little further north is the conspicuously modern business quarter Zona Azca, home to the city's tallest skyscraper – the 43-storey Torre Picasso (designed by Minoru Yamasaki, also architect of the former Twin Towers in New York).

Estadio Santiago Bernabéu

C/Concha Espina 1 ☎913 984 300, tickets ☎902 324 324, ⓦwww.real-madrid.com. Ticket office Mon–Fri 3–9pm (match days from 11am). Tickets from €30 go on sale a week before each match. Tour and trophy exhibition daily 10.30am–6.30pm; €9.

The magnificent Bernabéu stadium provides a suitably imposing home for the most glamorous team in football, Real Madrid. Venue of the 1982 World Cup final, the stadium has witnessed countless triumphs of "Los blancos", who have notched up 29 Spanish league titles and nine European Cup triumphs in their 102-year history. The arrival of Ronaldo, Zinedine Zidane, David Beckham and Michael Owen has helped complete an all-star line-up, dubbed "Los Galacticos"

▲ PASEO DE LA CASTELLANA

by the Spanish sports press. These superstar recruits mean that tickets have become increasingly difficult to get hold of, but Real do run a telephone booking service. The best technique when calling is to remain silent when asked questions by the automated system; you then get passed to an operator (most of whom speak English) who provide tickets more efficiently.

You can still catch a glimpse of the hallowed turf on the over-priced stadium tour during which you visit the changing rooms, walk around the edge of

the pitch and sit in the VIP box before heading to the trophy room with its endless cabinets of gleaming silverware. Note that tour schedules are disrupted on match days and when the team is training, so it's worth checking before you go.

Plaza Castilla

The Paseo de la Castellana ends with a flourish at Plaza Castilla with the dramatic leaning towers of the Puerta de Europa. Construction of the smoked-glass office blocks was financed by the Kuwait Investment Office (KIO) until the collapse of its Spanish subsidiary in one of the country's biggest-ever bankruptcies. The towers stood unfinished for several years until the powerful local bank Caja Madrid came to the rescue. All in all they provide a pretty fitting testimony to the uncontrolled property speculation of the 1980s.

Over the next 20 years the plan is to extend the Castellana another 3.5km northwards as part of the local authority's ambitious attempt to convert the area into one of Europe's major business centres.

Fundación Juan March

C/Castelló 77 ⓦwww.march.es. Mon–Fri 10am–2pm & 5.30–9pm, Sat & Sun 10am–2pm; closed Aug. Free. Founded in 1955 by a Catalan businessman seeking to make amends after spending time in prison for embezzlement, this outstanding cultural centre houses over 1300 works and is a venue for a variety of high quality art exhibitions and classical concerts.

Plaza de Toros de Las Ventas

C/Alcalá 237 ☎913 562 200, ⓦwww.las-ventas.com. Box office March–Oct Thurs–Sun 10am–2pm &

▲ REAL MADRID'S HOME GROUND

5–8pm; Caja Madrid ticket line ☎902 488 488 and from authorised agents in booths along c/Victoria near Sol. €5–110. Situated on the eastern-most tip of the Barrio de Salamanca, Madrid's 23,000-capacity, neo-Mudéjar bullring, Las Ventas, is the most illustrious in the world. The season lasts from March to October and *corridas* (bullfights) are held every Sunday at 7pm and every day during the three main *ferias*: La Comunidad (early May), San Isidro (mid-May to June) and Otoño (late Sept to Oct). Tickets go on sale at the ring a couple of days in advance, though many are already allocated to season-ticket holders. The cheapest seats are *gradas*, the highest rows at the back, from where you can see everything that happens without too much of the detail; the front rows are known as the *barreras*. Seats are also divided into *sol* (sun), *sombra* (shade) and *sol y sombra* (shaded after a while), with *sombra* seats the most expensive.

There's a taurine **museum** attached to the bullring (March–Oct Tues–Fri 9.30am–2.30pm, Sun & fight days 10am–1pm; Nov–Feb Mon–Fri 9.30am–2pm; free) with an intriguing if rather anarchic collection of bullfighting memorabilia including stunning *trajes de luces*, the beautifully deco-rated suits worn by the *toreros*.

Shops

ABC Serrano

Paseo de la Castellana 34 and c/Serrano 61 ⓦwww.abcserrano .com. Mon–Sat 10am–8pm. Upmarket shopping mall housed in the beautiful for-mer headquarters of the *ABC* newspaper. There's a wine store and fashion and household out-lets, as well as a couple of bars and restaurants.

Adolfo Domínguez

C/José Ortega y Gasset 4 Mon–Sat 10am–2pm & 5–8.30pm; c/Serrano 96 10am–8.30pm. Domínguez's clas-sic modern Spanish designs – subdued colours, free lines – are quite pricey but he does have a cheaper *Basico* range. Both branches have men's clothes; women's are only available at the Ortega y Gasset branch.

Agatha Ruiz de la Prada

C/Serrano 27. Mon–Sat 10am–8.30pm. *Movida*-era designer who shows and sells her brightly-coloured clothes and accessories at this out-let. There's a children's line, sta-tionery and household goods too.

Álvarez Gómez

C/Serrano 14 ⓦwww.alvarezgomez.com. Mon–Sat 10am–2pm & 5–8.30pm. Álvarez Gómez has been making the same perfumes in the same bot-tles for over a hundred years, with fragrances – carnation, rose and violet – that are as simple as they come. The elegant shop, complete with chandeliers, also sells stylish toilet bags, hats and umbrellas.

Area Real Madrid

C/Concha Espina 1 and Bernabéu Stadium. Mon–Sat 10am–8pm, Sun 11am–8pm (C/Concha Espina branch). Club store where you can pick up replica shirts of "galacticos" Beckham, Owen, Ronaldo, Zidane and all manner of – expensive – souvenirs related to the club's history.

▲ PUERTA DE EUROPA

Ekseptión

C/Velázquez 28. Mon–Sat 10.30am–2.30pm & 5–8.30pm. A dramatic catwalk bathed in spotlights leads into this shop selling some of the most expensive women's clothes in Madrid. Next door are younger, more casual clothes in the Eks shop for both men and women. There's also a branch selling discount last-season fashions at half price at Avda. Concha Espina 14 (Mon–Sat 11.30am–8pm).

Loewe

C/Serrano 26 & 34 ⓦwww.loewe.es. 9.30am–8.30pm. Luxury leather goods for men and women – including shoes, belts and bags – from this high-priced designer label

Sybilla

C/Jorge Juan 12. Mon–Sat 10am–2pm & 4.30–8.30pm. Spain's top designer of the 1980s, Sybilla remains at the forefront of the women's fashion scene – with prices to match. And if shopping gets too tiring, there are armchairs and sofas to collapse into.

Cafés

Café el Espejo

Paseo de Recoletos 31. Mon–Thurs & Sun 10am–2am, Fri & Sat 10am–3am. Opened in 1978, but you wouldn't guess it from the antiquated decor – mirrors, gilt and a wonderful, extravagant glass pavilion, plus a leafy outside *terraza*. An ideal spot to buy a coffee and watch the world go by.

Café Gijón

Paseo de Recoletos 21. Daily 8am–1.30am. Famous literary café dating from 1888, decked out in Cuban mahogany and mirrors. A centre of the *Movida* in the 1980s, it still hosts regular artistic *tertulias* (discussion groups). There's a cellar restaurant, a very pleasant summer *terraza* and a set menu at lunchtime.

Restaurants

El Amparo

Callejón Puigcerdá 8 ☎914 316 456. Mon–Fri 1.30–3.30pm & 9–11.30pm, Sat 9–11.30pm. Critics rate this designer restaurant among the top five in Madrid – and you'll need to book a couple of weeks ahead to get a table. If you strike lucky, the rewards are faultless Basque cooking, with mains around €25.

▲ DESIGNER CLOTHES SHOP, SALAMANCA

Hard Rock Café

Paseo de la Castellana 2 ☎914 364 340. Daily 12.30pm–2am. A children's favourite, with its tried-and-tested formula of rock memorabilia and burgers at under €20 a head. The best thing about it is the summer *terraza* overlooking Plaza Colón.

El Pescador

C/José Ortega y Gasset 75 ☎914 021 290. Mon–Sat 1–4pm & 9pm–midnight. Closed Aug. One of the city's top seafood restaurants, with specials flown in from the Atlantic each morning. The clientele can be a bit intimidating and so can the prices (around €45 a head), but you'll rarely experience better seafood cooking than this.

Suntory

Paseo de la Castellana 36 ☎915 773 733. Mon–Sat 1.30–3.30pm & 8.30–11.30pm. Closed hols. Authentic and upmarket Japanese restaurant with showy service, great presentation but small portions. The best idea is to go for the lunchtime set menu at €25, or you could try the *menú de degustación*, which gives you a sample of all the top dishes for €37.

La Trainera

C/Lagasca 60 ☎915 768 035. Mon–Sat 1–4pm & 8pm–midnight. Closed Aug. High-quality seafood place, popular with politicians and businessmen, with prices to match (bank on €40 a head). Seafood platters, very fresh fish and an excellent selection of wines.

Zalacaín

C/Álvarez de Baena 4 ☎915 614 840. Mon–Fri 1.15–4pm & 9pm–midnight, Sat 9pm–midnight. Closed Aug. Luxurious setting for one of the best – and most expensive – restaurants in town. Basque-style cooking from master chef Benjamín Urdaín, but you pay for the pleasure with a meal costing around €90 per person. Male customers must wear jackets.

Tapas bars

Alkalde

C/Jorge Juan 10. Daily noon–midnight. This place serves up pricey Basque tapas, a treat which you could turn into a tasty meal. Alternatively there's an expensive and rather overrated restaurant downstairs.

Hevia

C/Serrano 118. Mon–Sat 9am–1.30am. Plush venue and clientele for pricey but excellent tapas and canapés – the hot Camembert is delicious, as is the *surtido de ahumados* (selection of smoked fish).

José Luís

C/Serrano 89. Mon–Sat 9am–1am, Sun

▲ ZALACAÍN RESTAURANT

noon–11pm. The best of this chain of smart bar/restaurants, established by a Basque in the late 1950s. It serves dainty and delicious sandwiches, along with canapés of crab, black pudding and steak, but the bill quickly mounts up if you're not careful.

Bars

Teatriz

C/Hermosilla 15. Bar 9pm–3am, restaurant 1.30–4.30pm & 9pm–1am; closed Sat lunch, Sun & Aug. This former theatre, redesigned by Catalan designer Mariscal and Philippe Starck, is as elegant a club/bar/restaurant as any in Europe. There are bars on the main theatre levels, while down in the basement there's a library-like area and small disco. Drinks are pretty pricey (€9 for spirits) but there's no entrance charge.

Clubs and discobares

ABC Serrano

Paseo de la Castellana 34. Popular summer rooftop terrace on the fourth floor of this rather exclusive Salamanca shopping mall overlooking the Castellana.

Boulevard

Paseo de la Castellana 95. Daily 10pm–late. Expensive summer *terraza* popular with Madrileño *pijos* and *pijas* (rich kids). Gets more crowded and more posey as the night wears on.

Macumba Clubbing

Estación de Chamartín ☎902 499 994, ⓦwww.spaceofsound.net. Elite Noche: Sat midnight–6am. Space of Sound: Sun 9am–6pm. €15 including first drink. Guest DJs from London's Ministry of Sound come for the Saturday Elite Noche all-nighter and if you just can't stop till you get enough, the Space of Sound "after hours" club allows you to strut your stuff through Sunday too.

Vanitas Vanitatis

C/Velázquez 128. Mon–Thurs & Sun 8.30pm–3am, Fri & Sat 10pm–5am. Refurbished place that has been a popular nightspot on the Salamanca scene for the best part of a decade. Posey clientele and strict door policy.

Plaza de España and around

Largely constructed in the Franco era and dominated by two early Spanish skyscrapers, the Plaza de España provides an imposing full stop to Gran Vía and a breathing space from the densely packed streets to the east. Beyond the square lies a mixture of aristocratic suburbia, university campus and parkland, distinguished by the green swathes of Parque del Oeste and Casa de Campo. Sights include the eclectic collections of the Museo Cerralbo, the fascinating Museo de América, the Ermita de San Antonio de la Florida, with some stunning Goya frescoes and, further out, the pleasant royal residence of El Pardo, while the spacious *terrazas* along Paseo del Pintor Rosales provide ample opportunity for refreshment.

Plaza de España

The Plaza de España was the Spanish dictator Franco's attempt to portray Spain as a dynamic, modern country. The gargantuan apartment complex of the **Edificio de España**, which heads the square, looks like it was transplanted from 1920s New York, but was in fact completed in 1953. Four years later, the 32-storey **Torre de Madrid** took over as the tallest building in Spain. Together they tower over an elaborate **monument to Cervantes** in the middle of the square, set by an uninspiring pool. The plaza itself can be a little seedy at night, although it does play host to occasional festivities and an interesting craft fair during the fiesta of San Isidro (on or around May 15).

Museo de Cerralbo

C/Ventura Rodríguez 17 ⓦmuseocerralbo.mcu.es. Tues–Sat 9.30am–3pm, Sun & hols 10–3pm; July & Aug

Tues–Sat 9.30am–2pm, Sun & hols 11–2pm. Guided visits Tues, Thurs, Fri & Sat (reservations ☎915 473 646). Free guided visits Wed 11am & Sat noon. €2.40, free Wed & Sun. Reactionary politician, poet, traveller and archeologist, the seventeenth Marqués de Cerralbo endowed his elegant

▼ CERVANTER MONUMENT, PLAZA DE ESPAÑA

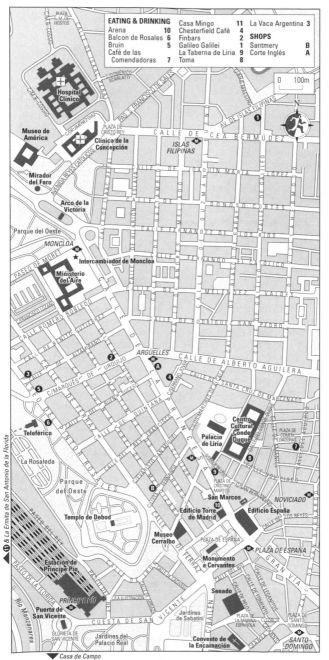

EATING & DRINKING
Arena 10
Balcon de Rosales 6
Bruin 5
Café de las
  Comendadoras 7
Casa Mingo 11
Chesterfield Café 4
Finbars 2
Galileo Galilei 1
La Taberna de Liria 9
Toma 8
La Vaca Argentina 3

SHOPS
Santmery B
Corte Inglés A

0   100m

N

Hospital
Clínico

Museo de
América

Mirador
del Faro

Arco de la
Victoria

Parque del Oeste

MONCLOA

Intercambiador de Moncloa

Ministerio
del Aire

Teleférico

La Rosaleda

Parque
del Oeste

Templo de Debod

Estación de
Príncipe Pío

PRÍNCIPE PÍO

Puerta de
San Vicente

Jardines del
Palacio Real

Casa de Campo

& La Ermita de San Antonio de la Florida

Río Manzanares

Clínica de la
Concepción

ISLAS
FILIPINAS

PLAZA
E.M.DE
HOSTOS

C.Mª DE COSSIO

PASEO JUAN XXIII

DOMÉNICO
SCARLATTI

AV. DE ISLAS FILIPINAS

CALLE DE CEA BERMÚDEZ

CALLE DE JOAQUÍN MARÍA LÓPEZ

CALLE DE FERNANDO EL CATÓLICO

CALLE DE RODRÍGUEZ SAN PEDRO

ARGUELLES

CALLE DE ALBERTO AGUILERA

C/MARQUÉS DE URQUIJO

C/QUINTANA

CALLE DE MARTÍN DE LOS HEROS

CALLE DE FERRAZ

PASEO DEL PINTOR ROSALES

CALLE DE SANTA CRUZ DE MARCENADO

Centro
Cultural
Conde
Duque

Palacio
de Liria

PLAZA DE
COMEN-
DADORAS

NOVICIADO

Edificio España

San Marcos

Edificio Torre
de Madrid

Museo
Cerralbo

PLAZA DE
CRISTINO
MARTOS

CALLE SAN BERNARDINO

PLAZA DE ESPAÑA

Monumento
a Cervantes

GRAN VÍA

Senado

CUESTA DE SAN VICENTE

Jardines
de Sabatini

Convento de
la Encarnación

PLAZA DE
LA MARINA
ESPAÑOLA

SANTO
DOMINGO

GLORIETA DE
SAN VICENTE

Jardines del
Palacio Real

nineteenth-century mansion with a substantial collection of paintings, furniture and armour. Bequeathed to the state on his death, the house opened as a museum in 1962 and the cluttered nature of the exhibits is partly explained by the fact that the marqués's will stipulated that objects should be displayed exactly as he had arranged them. The highlight is a fabulous over-the-top mirrored ballroom with a Tiepolo-inspired fresco, golden stucco work and marbled decoration.

Centro Cultural Conde Duque

C/Conde Duque 9–11. ⓦwww .munimadrid.es/condeduque. Tues–Sat 10am–2pm & 5.30–9pm, Sun & hols 10.30am–2.30pm. Free.
Constructed in the early eighteenth century, this former barracks of the royal guard has been converted into a dynamic cultural centre, housing the city's collection of contemporary art and hosting a variety of temporary exhibitions. It also stages an excellent series of concerts, plays and dance as part of

▼ CENTRO CULTURAL CONDE DUQUE

the local council's *Veranos de la Villa* season in the summer.

Plaza de Comendadoras

Bordered by a variety of interesting craft shops, bars and cafés, this tranquil square is named after the convent that occupies one side of it. The convent is run by nuns from the military order of Santiago and the attached church is decked out with banners celebrating the victories of the order's knights. A large painting of their patron, St James the Moor-slayer, hangs over the high altar. The plaza itself comes alive in the summer months when the *terrazas* open and locals gather for a chat and a drink.

El Ministerio del Aire

The Air Ministry is another product of the post–Civil War Francoist building boom. Work on the mammoth edifice began in 1942, and even the Third Reich's architect, Albert Speer, was consulted. However, with the defeat of the Nazis, plans were soon changed and a Habsburg-style structure was built instead, nicknamed the "Monasterio" del Aire because of its similarity to El Escorial. The neighbouring Arco de la Victoria was constructed in 1956 to commemorate the Nationalist military triumph in the Civil War.

Mirador del Faro

Tues–Sun 10am–2pm & 5–8pm. €1. At 92m high, this futuristic viewing tower provides stunning views over the city and to the mountains beyond. It's unfortunate

▲ MIRADOR DEL FARO

then that there are no explanation panels to identify what you're seeing.

Museo de América

Avenida de los Reyes Católicos 6. Tues–Sat 9.30am–3pm, Sun 10am–3pm. €3, free Sun. This fabulous collection of pre-Columbian American art and artefacts includes objects brought back at the time of the Spanish Conquest, as well as more recent acquisitions and donations. The layout is thematic, with sections on geography, history, social organization, religion and communication. The Aztec, Maya and Inca civilizations are well represented and exhibits include the Madrid Codex, one of only three surviving hieroglyphic manuscripts depicting everyday Maya life; the Tudela Codex, including indigenous paintings describing the events of the Spanish Conquest; and the Quimbayas Treasure, a breathtaking collection of gold objects from a funeral treasure of the Colombian Quimbaya culture, dated 900–600 BC.

Parque del Oeste

Featuring a pleasant stream, assorted statues and shady walks, this delightful park offers a welcome respite from the busy streets of the capital. In summer there are numerous *terrazas* overlooking it on Paseo del Pintor Rosales. The beautiful rose garden – in c/Rosaleda – is at its most fragrant in May and June, while further down the hill is a small cemetery where the 43 Spaniards executed by occupying French troops on May 3, 1808 – and immortalised by Goya in his famous painting in the Prado – lie buried.

Templo de Debod

@www.munimadrid.es/templodebod/. April–Sept Tues–Fri 10am–2pm & 6–8pm, Sat & Sun 10am–2pm; Oct–March Tues–Fri 9.45am–1.45pm & 4.15–6.15pm, Sat & Sun 10am–2pm. Free. A fourth-century BC Egyptian temple in the middle of Madrid may seem an incongruous sight. It's here, however, as a thank you from the Egyptian government for Spanish help in salvaging archeological sites threatened by the construction of the Aswan High Dam. Reconstructed here stone by stone in 1968, it has a multimedia exhibition on the culture of Ancient Egypt inside.

El Teleférico

Paseo del Pintor Rosales @www .teleferico.com/madrid. Easter to mid-

▼ QUIMBAYAS TREASURE, MUSEO DE AMÉRICA

PLACES

Plaza de España and around

▲ PARQUE DEL OESTE'S ROSE GARDEN

Sept daily noon–8pm; mid-Sept to Easter Sat, Sun & hols noon–6pm. €2.90 single, €4.20 return. Running from the edge of the Parque del Oeste is the Teleférico, a cable car that shuttles its passengers high over the Manzanares River to a restaurant/bar in the middle of Casa de Campo (see opposite). The round trip offers some fine views of the park, the Palacio Real, the Almudena Cathedral and the city skyline.

La Ermita de San Antonio de la Florida

Paseo de la Florida 5 ⊛www.muni-madrid.es/ermita. Tues–Fri 10am–2pm & 4–8pm, Sat & Sun 10am–2pm; July 13–23 closed pm. Free. Built on a Greek-cross plan between 1792 and 1798, this little church is the burial site of Goya and also features some outstanding frescoes by him. Those in the recently restored dome depict St Anthony of Padua resurrecting a dead man to give evidence in favour of a prisoner (the saint's father) unjustly accused of murder. The mirror-image chapel on the other side of the road was built in 1925 for parish services so that the original could become a museum. On St Anthony's Day (June 13) girls queue at the church to ask the saint for a boyfriend; if pins dropped into the holy water then stick to their hands, their wish will be granted.

Casa de Campo

The Casa de Campo, an enormous expanse of heath and scrub, is in parts surprisingly wild for a place so easily accessible from the city. Founded by Felipe II in the mid-sixteenth century as a royal hunting estate, it was only opened to the public in 1931 and soon after acted as a base for Franco's forces to shell the city. Large sections have been tamed for conventional pastimes and there are picnic tables and café/bars throughout the park, the ones by the lake providing fine views of the city. There are also mountain-bike trails, a jogging track, an open-air swimming pool (June–Sept daily 10.30am–8pm; €3.40), tennis courts, and rowing boats for rent on the lake, all near Metro Lago.

The park is best avoided after dark as many of its roads are frequented by prostitutes.

Zoo-Aquarium

Casa de Campo ☎917 119 950, ⊛www.zoomadrid.com. Daily 10.30am–dusk. €13.10. Laid out in sections corresponding to the five continents, Madrid's zoo, on the southwestern edge of Casa de Campo, provides decent enclosures and plenty of space for over 2000 different species. When you've had your fill of big cats, koalas and venomous snakes, you can check out the aquarium, dolphinarium, children's zoo or bird show. Boats can be rented and there are train tours too.

Parque de Atracciones

Casa de Campo ☎915 268 030 or 914 632 900, ⊕www.parquedeatracciones.es. June–Sept daily noon–midnight, Fri & Sat till 1am; Oct–June Fri–Sun & hols noon–dusk, Sat till 1am. €5.70; entry with unlimited access to rides (Calco Adulto) €21.80. Madrid's most popular theme park, where highlights include the 63-metre vertical drop, La Lanzadera, the stomach-churning La Máquina, the whitewater raft ride, Los Rápidos, and the haunted house, El Viejo Caserón. Spanish acts perform in the open-air auditorium in the summer and there are frequent parades too, plus plenty of burger/pizza places to replace lost stomach contents.

El Pardo

C/Manuel Alonso ⊕www.patrimonionacional.es. April–Sept Mon–Sat 10.30am–6pm, Sun 9.30am–1.30pm; Oct–March Mon–Sat 10.30am–5pm, Sun 10am–1.30pm; closed for official visits. Guided tours €5, free Wed for EU citizens. Buses from Moncloa (daily 6.30am–midnight; every 10–15min; 25min) make the nine-kilometre journey north-west of central Madrid to Franco's former principal residence at El Pardo. A garrison still remains at the town, where most of the Generalíssimo's staff were based, but the place is now a popular excursion for Madrileños, who come here for long lunches at the excellent *terraza* restaurants.

The tourist focus is the **Palacio del Pardo**, rebuilt by the Bourbons on the site of the hunting lodge of Carlos I and still used by visiting heads of state. Behind the imposing but blandly symmetrical facade, the interior houses the chapel where Franco prayed, and the theatre where he used to censor films. On display are a number of mementos of the dictator, including his desk, a portrait of Isabel la Católica and an excellent collection of tapestries. Tickets to the palace are also valid for the neighbouring pavilion, the Casita del Príncipe (currently being refurbished).

Shops

Santmery

C/Juan Álvarez Mendizábal 27. Mon–Fri 9.30am–3pm & 5.30–10pm, Sat

▼ TEMPLO DE DEBOD

▲ VIEW FROM CASA DE CAMPO

9.30am–3pm. Fascinating wine shop that also doubles as a bar and delicatessen. You can sample some of the wines by the glass, while more exclusive ones have to be bought by the bottle. Try some of the top-quality cheese and ham too, or even the house speciality *mousse de cabrales a la sidra* (blue cheese and cider paté).

El Corte Inglés

C/Princesa 41 & 56. Mon–Sat 10am–10pm. One of many branches of Spain's biggest and most popular department store. It stocks everything from souvenirs and gift items to clothes and electrical goods. Prices are on the high side, but quality is usually very good.

Cafés

Bruin

Paseo Pintor Rosales 48. Daily noon–1am. Old-fashioned ice-cream parlour – serving 35 different varieties – that makes a good stop-off point before heading into nearby Parque del Oeste. Iced drinks are also on sale and there's a very pleasant summer terrace too.

Café de las Comendadoras

Plaza de las Comendadoras 1. Daily: winter 6pm–2am; summer noon–2am. Relaxing café with a buzzing summer *terraza*, situated on one of the city's nicest squares.

Restaurants

Casa Mingo

Paseo de la Florida 2 ☎915 477 918. Daily 11am–midnight. Closed Aug. Noisy, crowded and reasonably priced Asturian chicken-and-cider house. Tables are like gold dust, so loiter with your bottle of *sidra* in hand. The spit-roast chicken is practically compulsory, though the *chorizo* cooked in cider and *cabrales* (blue cheese) is also very good. Well worth the €15 a head.

La Taberna de Liria

C/Duque de Liria 9 ☎915 414 519. Mon–Fri 1–3.30pm & 9.15–11.30pm, Sat 9.15–11.30pm. Closed Aug. Imaginative Mediterranean-style dishes with a French touch. Great fish, inventive salads and excellent desserts, though pricey at around €40 a head.

Toma

C/Conde Duque 14 ☎915 474 996. Tues–Sat 9pm–12.30am. Intimate little restaurant with just a handful of tables in a bright red room, where husband and wife team Paul and Angela serve up a constantly changing menu with a creative twist. Booking is essential and budget on €25–30 a head.

La Vaca Argentina

Paseo del Pintor Rosales 52 ☎915 596 605. Daily 1–5pm & 9pm–midnight. Great Argentinian restaurant, serving tasty grilled steaks (*churrasco*) and with good views of the Parque del Oeste from its summer terrace. Average cost is around €25.

▲ PARQUE DE ATRACCIONES

Bars

Balcón de Rosales

Paseo Pintor Rosales ⊛www .balconderosales.com. Summer: Tues–Sat 8pm–late; winter: Thurs–Sat 8pm–late. Very popular summer venue complete with cocktail bar, disco, Tex-Mex restaurant and karaoke. Give the restaurant a miss but try a cocktail on the cool terrace overlooking the Parque del Oeste.

Finbars

C/Marqués de Urquijo 10. Mon–Fri 10.30am–1.30am, Sat & Sun noon–2am. Pub sports and Guinness in this friendly Irish bar on an attractive street close to the Parque del Oeste.

Clubs and discobares

Arena

C/Princesa 1 ⊛www.salarena.com. Thurs midnight–5am, Fri–Sat 7.30–11.30pm & midnight–6am. Entry around €11. Big, modern and very popular disco, which is also used as an occasional concert venue. There are early evening sessions at the weekends for teenagers, but the serious stuff starts well after midnight.

Chesterfield Café

C/Serrano Jover 5. Daily 1.30pm–3am. Tex-Mex food, cocktails, international parties and regular concerts (for which you pay) at this America-style club/restaurant.

Galileo Galilei

C/Galileo 100 ⊛www.salagalileo-galilei.com. Daily 6pm–4.30am. €4–10. Bar, concert venue and disco rolled into one. Latin music is regularly on offer, along with cabaret and flamenco.

El Escorial and Valle de los Caídos

Fifty kilometres northwest of Madrid, in the foothills of the Guadarrama mountains, lies one of Spain's most visited sights – Felipe II's immense monastery-palace complex of El Escorial. Built between 1563 and 1584 by Juan Bautista de Toledo and Juan de Herrera, the monk-like Felipe planned the austere strcuture as monastery, mausoleum and palace. The result dominates the surrounding town and provides an unprecedented insight into the mindset of Spain's greatest king. Some 9km further north and easily visited from El Escorial, El Valle de los Caídos (The Valley of the Fallen) is an equally megalomaniacal, yet far more chilling monument: an underground basilica hewn under Franco's orders, allegedly to commemorate the Civil War dead of both sides, though in reality a memorial to the Generalíssimo and his regime.

EL Escorial

El Escorial was the largest Spanish building of the Renaissance, built to celebrate a victory over the French in 1557 and divided into different sections for either secular or religious use. Linking the two zones is the **Biblioteca** (Library), a splendid hall with vivid, multicoloured frescoes by Tibaldi. The library's collections include Santa Teresa's personal diary, some gorgeously executed Arabic manuscripts and a Florentine planetarium of 1572 demonstrating the movement of the planets. Beyond is the Patio de los Reyes, named after the six statues of the kings of Israel which adorn the facade of the Basílica, on the far side of the courtyard.

Visiting El Escorial

There are up to 31 **trains** a day to El Escorial from Madrid (5.45am–11.30pm from Atocha, calling at Chamartín), or **buses** #661 and #664 from the *intercambiador* at Moncloa run every fifteen minutes on weekdays and hourly at weekends.

Opening hours of the complex are Tues–Sun: April–Sept 10am–6pm; Oct–March 10am–5pm. Tickets cost €8 non-guided, €9 guided; combined ticket with El Valle de los Caídos €8.50 non-guided, €10 guided; free Wed for EU citizens.

The helpful **oficina de turismo** (Mon–Thurs 11am–6pm, Fri–Sun 10am–7pm; ☏918 905 313, ⓦwww.sanlorenzodeelescorial.org) is at c/Grimaldi 2.

To visit **El Valle de los Caídos** from El Escorial, there's a local bus run by Herranz (#660), which starts from their office in Plaza de la Virgen de Gracia. The bus runs from El Escorial at 3.15pm, returning at 5.30pm (Tues–Sun; €7.80 return including entrance to the monument).

▲ EL ESCORIAL

The enormous, cold, dark interior of the **Basílica** contains over forty altars, designed to allow simultaneous Masses to be held. Behind the main altar lies some of Felipe's mammoth collection of saintly relics, including six whole bodies, over sixty heads and hundreds of bone fragments set in fabulously expensive caskets.

You can also wander round some of El Escorial's courtyards including the Claustro Grande with its Tibaldi frescoes depicting the life of the Virgin, and the secluded gardens of the Patio de los Evangelistas that lie within.

Many of the monastery's religious treasures are contained in the **Sacristía** and **Salas Capitulares** (Chapter Houses) and include paintings by Titian, Velázquez and José Ribera.

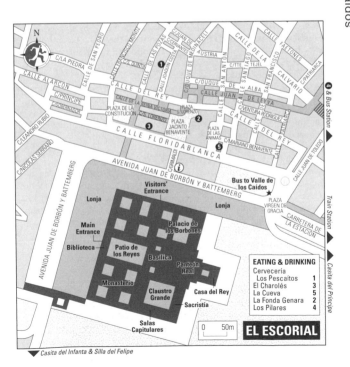

EATING & DRINKING
Cervecería Los Pescaítos	1
El Charolés	3
La Cueva	5
La Fonda Genara	2
Los Pilares	4

EL ESCORIAL

0   50m

Casita del Infanta & Silla del Felipe

▲ LIBRARY IN EL ESCORIAL

Below these rooms is the Panteón Real, where past Spanish monarchs lie in their gilded marble tombs. The royal children are laid in the Panteón de los Infantes and there's also a babies' tomb with room for sixty infants.

What remains of El Escorial's art collection – works by Bosch, Dürer, Titian, Zurbarán, among others that escaped transfer to the Prado – is kept in the elegant Museos Nuevos. Don't miss the Sala de Batallas, a long gallery lined with an epic series of paintings depicting important imperial battles. Finally, there are the treasure-crammed Salones Reales (Royal Apartments), containing the austere quarters of Felipe II, with the chair that supported his gouty leg and the deathbed from which he was able to contemplate the high altar of the Basílica.

Casita del Príncipe and Casita del Infante

The outlying lodges of the complex, the Casita del Príncipe (aka Casita de Abajo; June–Sept

Sat & Sun 10am–1pm & 4–6.30pm; €3.60; tours only, every 30min; reservations ☎918 905 903) and the Casita del Infante (aka Casita de Arriba; Easter & mid-July to mid-Sept Tues–Sun 10am–6.45pm; €3.40, free Wed for EU citizens) are two eighteenth-century royal lodges, both full of decorative riches, and built by Juan de Villanueva, Spain's most accomplished Neoclassical architect. Their greatest appeal, however, lies in wandering through their delightful formal gardens.

La Silla de Felipe

Around 3km out of town, is the Silla de Felipe – "Felipe's Seat" – a chair carved into a rocky outcrop with a great view of the palace, and from where the king is supposed to have watched the building's construction. You can reach it on foot by following the path through the arches beyond the main entrance to the monastery by the Biblioteca; keep to the left as you go down the hill and then cross the main road and follow the signs. If you have a car, take the M-505 Ávila road and turn off at the sign after about 3km.

Valle de los Caídos

Tues–Sun: April–Sept 10am–6pm; Oct–March 10am–5pm. €5, combined ticket with El Escorial €8.50 unguided, €10 guided, free Wed for EU citizens. Almost at first glance, this basilica complex, constructed by Franco after his Civil War victory, belies its claim to be a memorial to the dead of both sides. The dour, pompous architectural forms employed, the constant inscriptions "Fallen for God and for Spain", and the proximity to El Escorial clue you in to its true function – the glorification of General Franco and his regime. The dictator himself lies buried behind the high altar, while the only other named tomb is that of his guru, the Falangist leader, José Antonio Primo de Rivera. The "other side" is present only in the fact that the whole thing was built by the Republican army's survivors.

From the entrance to the basilica, a shaky funicular (Tues–Sun: April–Sept 11am–1.30pm & 4–6pm; Oct–March 11am–1.30pm & 3–5.30pm; €2.50) ascends to the base of a vast cross, reputedly the largest in the world, offering superlative views over the Sierra de Guadarrama and of the giant, grotesque religious figures propping up the cross.

Restaurants

Cervecería Los Pescaítos

C/Joaquín Costa 8, El Escorial ☎918 907 720. Daily 1–4pm & 8pm–midnight. A friendly and very popular local bar serving great fish dishes and good wine. Tapas cost from €8–10 and a full meal around €20–25 a head.

El Charolés

C/Floridablanca 24, El Escorial ☎918 905 975. Daily 1–4pm & 9pm–midnight. Prestigious restaurant renowned for its fish and stews. They serve a warming *cocido* in winter on Wednesdays and Fridays. Around €30 per person.

La Cueva

C/San Antón 4, El Escorial ☎918 901 516, ⓦwww.mesonlacueva.com. Tues–Sun 10.30am–midnight. A good bet for both tapas and typical Castilian roasts, all at approximately €25 for a full meal.

La Fonda Genara

Plaza de San Lorenzo 2, El Escorial ☎918 904 357. Daily 1.30–4pm & 9.15–11.30pm. Low-key but highly enjoyable place, filled with theatrical mementos, and offering a wide range of good quality Castilian fare. *Menús* available for €10–13, otherwise around €30 per person.

Los Pilares

C/Juan de Toledo 58, El Escorial ☎918 961 972, ⓦwww.lospilares.com. Mon–Sat 1–4pm & 9–11.30pm, Sun 1–4pm. Near the bus station, this place specializes in re-creating dishes from the era of Felipe II – try the capon and bean stew. Over €30 per person.

▼ VALLE DE LOS CAÍDOS

Aranjuez and Chinchón

On the edge of the parched plains of New Castille, around 50 kilometres from the capital, is the little oasis town of Aranjuez. Situated at the confluence of the Tajo and Jarama rivers, this is where the eighteenth-century Bourbon rulers set up a spring and autumn retreat. Its opulent palaces and luxuriant gardens inspired composer Joaquín Rodrigo to write the famous *Concierto de Aranjuez*, while the summer *fresas con nata* (strawberries with cream), served at roadside stalls, make it a favourite weekend escape for Madrileños.

Nearby is picturesque Chinchón, a small village centred around an atmospheric old plaza lined with traditional *mesones* serving quality Castilian food. It's also home to Spain's best-known *anís* – a mainstay of breakfast drinkers across the country.

The Palacio Real

☎918 910 740, ⓦwww .patrimonionacional.es. Tues–Sun: April–Sept 10am–6.15pm; Oct–March 10am–5.15pm. €5, free Wed for EU citizens. The centrepiece of Aranjuez is the Palacio Real and its gardens (see p.139). Although there has been a royal residence on this site since the late sixteenth century, the present building dates from the 1700s and was an attempt by

Spain's Bourbon monarchs to create a Spanish Versailles. It isn't in the same league as its French counterpart but is still a pleasant place to while away a few hours and its three-sided courtyard entrance is impressive enough. The palace is noted more, however, for the ornamental fantasies inside than for any virtues of architecture. The seemingly endless number of rooms are all

Visiting Aranjuez and Chinchón

From the end of April to July and Sept to mid-Oct, a weekend service on an old wooden steam **train**, the Tren de la Fresa, runs between Madrid and Aranjuez. It leaves Atocha station at 10.05am and departs from Aranjuez at 6pm (information ☎902 228 822). The €22 fare includes a guided bus tour in Aranjuez, entry to the monuments and *fresas con nata* on the train. Standard trains leave every 15–30 minutes from Atocha, with the last train returning from Aranjuez at about 11.30pm.

Buses run every half-hour during the week and every hour at weekends from Estación Sur.

You'll find a helpful **oficina de turismo** in the Casa de Infantes (daily 10am–7.30pm, Oct–May closes 6pm; ☎918 910 427, ⓦwww.aranjuez.com).

There are hourly buses (#337) from Madrid to Chinchón from the bus station at Avda Mediterraneo 49 near the Plaza Conde Casal, or you can reach the village from Aranjuez on the sporadic service from c/Almíbar 138 (Mon–Fri 4 daily, Sat 2 daily). There's a small **turismo** in the Plaza Mayor (Mon–Fri 10am–8pm, Sat & Sun 11.30am–8pm; ☎918 935 323, ⓦwww.ciudad-chinchon.com).

exotically furnished, especially the Porcelain Room, entirely covered in decorative ware from the factory which once stood in Madrid's Retiro park. The Smoking Room is a copy of one of the finest halls of the Alhambra in Granada, though executed with less subtlety.

Jardín de la Isla and Jardín del Príncipe

Daily: April–Sept 8am–8.30pm; Oct–March 8am–6.30pm; free, audio guide €2. Two palace gardens worthy of a visit are the Jardín de la Isla with its fountains and neatly tended gardens on a small island, and the more attractive Jardín del Príncipe, on the other side of the main road, offering shaded walks along the river and plenty of spots for a siesta.

Casa del Labrador

Jardín del Príncipe. Tues–Sun: June–Sept 10am–6.15pm; Oct–March 10am–5.15pm; visits by appointment only ☎918 910 305. €5, free Wed for EU citizens. At the far end of the Jardín del Príncipe is the Casa del Labrador (Peasant's House), which is anything but what its name implies. The house contains more silk, marble, crystal and gold than would seem possible to cram into so small a place, as well as a huge collection of fancy clocks. Although the hotchpotch of styles will offend purists, this miniature palace still provides a fascinating

▲ ARANJUEZ'S PALACIO REAL

insight into the tastes of the Bourbon dynasty and the obligatory guided tour goes into great detail about the weight and value of every item.

Casa de los Marinos

Tues–Sun: April–Sept 10am–6.15pm; Oct–March 10am–5.15pm. €3.40, free Wed for EU citizens. The small Casa de los Marinos, or Museo de Faluas, is a museum containing the brightly coloured launches in which royalty would take to the river. You can do the modern equivalent and take a 45-minute boat trip through the royal parks from the jetty by the bridge next to the palace (summer: Tues–Sun 11am–sunset; €7).

Plaza de Toros

Tues–Sun: summer 11am–7.30pm; winter Tues–Sun 11am–5.30pm. €3, free Wed for EU citizens. Aranjuez's beautiful eighteenth-century Plaza de Toros houses a modest exhibition space entitled *Aranjuez – una gran fiesta*. Part of the exhibition holds a bull-fighting museum with *trajes de luces*, swords and associated memorabilia; the other part traces the town's history and royal heritage. Nearby, look out for c/Naranja and c/Rosa, which contain a number of *corrales*, traditional-style wooden-balconied tenement blocks.

Chinchón

A gentle stroll around the elegant little town of Chinchón, followed by a big lunch at one of its restaurants is a popular pastime for Madrileños. Noteworthy monuments include a fifteenth-century castle (not open to visitors), a picture-postcard medieval Plaza Mayor, and the Iglesia de la Asunción, with a panel by Goya of *The Assumption of the Virgin*, but it is as the home of **anís** that the town is best known. To sample the local aniseed spirit try one of the local bars or the Alcoholera de Chinchón, a shop on the Plaza Mayor – most visitors come for a tasting before eating at one of the town's traditional *mesones* (see p.142).

If you're visiting over Easter, you'll be treated to Chinchón's own enactment of the Passion of Christ, though be aware that the town becomes packed with visitors at this time.

In 1995 the town launched its *Fiesta del Anís y del Vino*, an orgy of *anís* and wine tasting, that, understandably, was an immediate success and is now held mid-April every year. An older annual tradition takes place on July 25, when the feast of St James (*Santiago* in Spanish) is celebrated with a bullfight in the Plaza Mayor.

▼ CASA DEL LABRADOR

Restaurants

Casa José

C/Abastos 32, Aranjuez
☎918 911 488. Tues–Sat 1.30–4pm & 8pm–midnight, Sun 1.30–4pm. Tasty but

expensive cuisine at this upmarket restaurant. The house speciality is stuffed artichokes, but all the dishes are given a creative twist. Expect to spend €40 per person.

Casa Pablo

C/Almíbar 42, Aranjuez ☎918 911 451. Daily 1–4pm & 8pm–midnight. Closed August. A traditional place, the walls of which are covered with pictures of local dignitaries and bullfighters, serving good-value main courses that bring the bill to around €30 per person.

Casa de Pregonero

Plaza Mayor 4, Chinchón ☎918 940 696, ⊛www.lacasadelpregonero.com. Mon & Wed–Sun 1–4pm & 8pm–midnight. Modern touches to traditional dishes, with some great starters and desserts too. The decent-value *menú del día* is €16.80 but à la carte will set you back €35–40 a head.

Mesón El Comendador

Plaza Mayor 21, Chinchón ☎918 940 420. Mon, Tues & Thurs–Sun: winter 11am–midnight; summer 11–4pm & 7pm–midnight. One of the best of a cluster of good restaurants overlooking the beautiful Plaza Mayor, serving classic Castilian fare. Prices around €30 a head.

Mesón Cuevas del Vino

C/Benito Hortelano 13, Chinchón ☎918 940 206, ⊛www.cuevasdelvino.com. Mon & Wed–Sun 1–4pm & 8pm–midnight. An old olive oil mill which has its own *bodega* (wine cellar) and was a favourite haunt of Orson Welles when he was filming *Chimes at Midnight* here in 1966. You'll need to book at weekends as it's very popular. Excellent roast lamb and *cochinillo* (suckling pig) and some superb starters, all of which will set you back €35–40.

El Rana Verde

Plaza Santiago Rusiñol, Aranjuez ☎918 911 571, ⊛www.aranjuez.com/ranaverde. Daily 8am–midnight. Probably the best-known restaurant in Aranjuez, this pleasant riverside establishment dates back to the late nineteenth century and serves a wide-ranging *menú* at around €13.

Tapas bars

Casa Pablete

C/Stuart 108, Aranjuez. Mon & Wed–Sun 1–4pm & 8pm–midnight. Closed Aug. An offshoot of *Casa Pablo* and one of the best places in town for tapas. Good beer and vermouth too.

▼ CHINCHÓN'S PLAZA MAYOR

Toledo

Set atop a massive outcrop, every available inch of which is covered in churches, synagogues, mosques and houses that cobbled lanes infiltrate as best they can, Toledo is one of Spain's most fascinating cities. A former capital, it's surrounded on three sides by the Río Tajo, and was immortalized by El Greco, who lived and worked here for most of his later career. The city itself is a showcase for the many cultures – Visigothic, Moorish, Jewish and Christian – that have shaped the destiny of Spain and here left behind a host of sights from the Alcázar that looms over the whole town, to the beautiful cathedral almost hidden in the dense web of medieval streets. Though Toledo often seems overrun with visitors, if you have time for just one day-trip from Madrid, this should be it. Even better, if you spend the night (see pp.165–166), you'll be able to enjoy the city's atmosphere without the crowds.

The Alcázar

C/Carlos V. Closed for refurbishment until 2007. If one building dominates Toledo, it's the bluff, imposing fortress of the Alcázar. The present building was started by Carlos V in the sixteenth century, though it has been burned and bombarded so often that almost nothing remaining is original. The most recent destruction was in 1936 during the Civil War, when Nationalist forces, besieged inside by the Republican town, were

▼ TOLEDO'S ALCÁZAR

Visiting Toledo

There are **buses** to Toledo from the Estación Sur in Madrid every 30 minutes, taking about 1hr 15min. The city's bus station is in the modern, lower part of the city; bus #5 runs from it to central Plaza de Zocódover. **Trains** run every 30–60min from Atocha; the journey is about 1hr 30min. Toledo's train station is about a twenty-minute walk or a bus ride (#5 or #6) from the heart of town.

The main **tourist office** (Mon–Sat 9am–7pm, winter Mon–Fri closes 6pm, Sun & hols 9am–3pm; ☏925 220 843, ⊛www.castillalamancha.es/clmturiocio) is outside the city walls opposite the Puerta Nueva de Bisagra. There's another office in the Zococentro shop at c/Sillería 16 in the centre and a small information kiosk in the plaza next to the cathedral (Mon 10.30am–2.30pm, Tues–Sun 10.30am–2.30pm & 4.30–7pm).

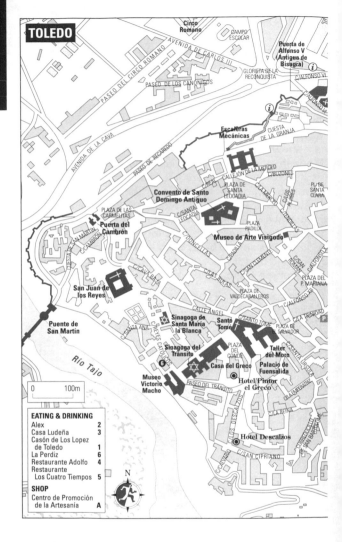

TOLEDO

EATING & DRINKING
Alex	2
Casa Ludeña	3
Casón de Los Lopez de Toledo	1
La Perdiz	6
Restaurante Adolfo	4
Restaurante Los Cuatro Tiempos	5

SHOP
Centro de Promoción de la Artesanía	A

eventually relieved by an army heading for Madrid, which then took severe retribution on the town.

After the war, Franco's regime completely rebuilt the Alcázar as a monument to its Civil War defenders.

The interior is currently undergoing a lengthy refurbishment to convert it into a new Army Museum that will eventually provide a home for all the exhibits once housed in the Madrid branch (see p.100).

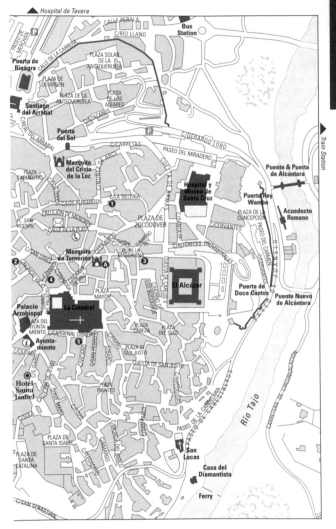

Hospital y Museo de Santa Cruz

C/Cervantes 3. Mon 10am–2pm &
4–6.30pm, Tues–Sat 10am–6.30pm,
Sun 10am–2pm. €1.25, free Sat pm
& Sun and during renovations. A
superlative Renaissance
building with a magnificent
Plateresque main doorway, this
museum houses some of the
greatest El Grecos in Toledo,
including *The Coronation of the
Virgin* and *The Assumption of the
Virgin*. As well as outstanding
works by Goya and Ribera,
there's also a huge collection of

ancient carpets and faded tapestries, a military display, sculpture, ceramics and a small archeological collection.

The Cathedral

C/Cardenal Cisneros. Mon–Sat 10.30am–6.30pm, Sun 2–6pm. Coro closed Sun am; museums closed Mon. €4.95, free Wed pm for EU citizens; audio guides €3. Toledo's stunning cathedral reflects the importance of the city that for so long outshone its near neighbour, Madrid. A robust Gothic construction, which took over two hundred and fifty years (1227–1493) to complete, it's richly decorated in almost every conceivable style from these years, with masterpieces of the Gothic, Renaissance and Baroque periods. The cavernous interior is home to some magnificent stained glass, an outstanding Coro (Choir), a wonderfully Gothic Capilla Mayor (Main Chapel) and an extravagant high altar. There are also well over twenty chapels embedded in the walls, many containing fine tombs. The cathedral museums are worth a look for their impressive collections including paintings by El Greco, Goya and Velázquez, as well as one of El Greco's few surviving pieces of sculpture.

Convento de Santo Domingo Antiguo

Plaza Santo Domingo Antiguo. Summer: Mon–Sat 11am–1.30pm & 4–7pm, Sun 4–7pm; winter: Sat, Sun & hols only. €1.50. The Convento de Santo Domingo Antiguo's chief claim to fame is as the resting place of El Greco, whose remains lie in the crypt that can be glimpsed through a peephole in the floor. The convent's religious treasures are displayed in the old choir, but more interesting is the high altarpiece of the church – El Greco's first major commission in Toledo. Unfortunately, most of the canvases have gone to museums and are here replaced by copies.

Santo Tomé and the Burial of the Count of Orgaz

Plaza del Conde ⓦwww.santotome.org. Daily: summer 10am–6.45pm; winter 10am–5.45pm. €1.50, free Wed after 2.30pm for EU citizens. Housed, alone, in a small annexe of the church of Santo Tomé, one of the most celebrated attractions of Toledo is El Greco's masterpiece, *The Burial of the Count of Orgaz*. The painting depicts the count's funeral, at which St Stephen and St Augustine appeared in order to lower him into the tomb. Combining El Greco's genius for the mystic with his great powers as a portrait painter and master of colour, the work includes a depiction of the artist himself – he can be spotted seventh from the left, looking out at the viewer with his son in the foreground. A search for the count's bones

▼ TOLEDO'S CATHEDRAL

came to an end in early 2001 when they were unearthed from a tomb located, appropriately enough, directly below the painting.

Casa y Museo del Greco

C/Samuel Levi. Tues–Sat 10am–2pm & 4–9pm, Sun 10am–2pm. €2.40. Despite its name, El Greco's House was never the artist's home. The building in fact dates from the beginning of the twentieth century and evidence suggests that he actually lived nearby. Nonetheless, the living quarters of the interior are furnished in sixteenth-century style and the museum part of the house displays many classic El Grecos, among them his famous *View and Map of Toledo*, and another full series of the Twelve Apostles, completed later than the set in the cathedral and subtly different in style.

▲ TOLEDO'S JEWISH QUARTER

▼ EL GRECO'S *VIEW OF TOLEDO*

Sinagoga del Tránsito

C/Samuel Levi ⊛www.museosefardi .net. Tues–Sat 10am–2pm & 4–9pm, Sun 10am–2pm. €2.40. Built along Moorish lines by Samuel Levi in 1366, the Sinagoga del Tránsito became a church after the fifteenth-century expulsion of the Jews and was restored to its original form only in the last century. The interior is a simple galleried hall, brilliantly decorated with polychromed stuccowork and superb filigree windows, while Hebrew inscriptions praising God, King Pedro and Samuel Levi adorn the walls. It also houses a small but engaging Sephardic Museum (same hours) tracing the distinct traditions and development of Jewish culture in Spain.

Sinagoga Santa María la Blanca

C/Reyes Católicos 4. Daily: summer 10am–7pm; winter 10am–6pm. €1.50. The second of Toledo's two surviving synagogues, the fascinating and tranquil Santa María la Blanca predates the Sinagoga del Tránsito by over a century. Despite having been both a church and synagogue, the horseshoe arches and the fact that it was built by Mudéjar craftsmen mean it actually looks most like a mosque. The arches are decorated with elaborate plaster designs of pine cones and palm trees, while a fine Baroque retablo (altarpiece) dates fom the time it was a church. The whole effect is stunning, all set off against a deep-red floor that contains some of the original decorative tiles.

San Juan de los Reyes

C/San Juan de los Reyes 2. Daily: summer 10am–6.45pm; winter 10am–5.45pm. €1.50. The exterior of this beautiful church is bizarrely festooned with the chains worn by the Christian prisoners from Granada released on the reconquest of the city in 1492. It was originally a Franciscan convent founded by the Reyes Católicos (Catholic Monarchs), Fernando and Isabel – who completed the Christian reconquest of Spain – and in which, until the fall of Granada, they had planned to be buried. Its double-storeyed cloister is outstanding, with an elaborate Mudéjar ceiling in the upper floor.

▼ MEZQUITA CRISTO DE LUZ

Mezquita del Cristo de la Luz

Cuesta de los Carmelitas Descalzos 10. Daily: summer 10am–7pm; winter 10am–6pm. €1.50. Although this is one of the oldest Moorish monuments in Spain (the mosque was built by Musa Ibn Ali in the tenth century on the foundations of a Visigothic church), only the nave, with its nine different cupolas, is the original Arab construction. The apse was added when the building was converted into a church, and is claimed to be the first product of the Mudéjar style. The mosque itself, set in a tiny patio-like park and open on all sides to the elements, is so small that it seems more like a miniature summer pavilion, but it has an elegant simplicity of design that few of the town's great monuments can match.

Hospital de Tavera

C/Cardenal Tavera 2. Daily 10.30am–1.30pm & 3.30–6pm. €3. A Renaissance palace with beautiful twin patios, the Hospital de Tavera houses the private collection of the Duke of Lerma. The rather gloomy interior is a reconstruction of a sixteenth-century mansion dotted with many fine paintings, while the museum contains several works by El Greco and Ribera's bizarre portrait of a "bearded woman".

Shops

Centro de Promoción de la Artesanía

C/Tornerías. Tues–Sat 10am–2pm & 5–8pm, Sun 10am–2pm. Housed in an old mosque, the Mezquita de las Tornerías, this shop/gallery houses interesting displays of beautiful local crafts, mainly pottery. The renovated eleventh-

▲ FACADE OF HOSPITAL TAVERA

century building, deconsecrated by the Reyes Católicos around 1500, is worth a visit in itself.

Restaurants

Alex

Plaza de Amador de los Ríos 10, at the top end of c/Nuncio Viejo. Reasonable-value restaurant with a much cheaper café attached. *Conejo* (rabbit) and *perdiz* (partridge) are the specialities. Nice location and a shady summer terrace. Around €25 per person.

Casa Ludeña

Plaza Magdalena 13. One of many places around this square, this one offers a cheap €9 *menú* and the best *carcamusa* (traditional meat stew in a spicy tomato sauce) in town.

Casón de Los López de Toledo

C/Sillería 3. Daily 1.30–4pm & 8.30–11.30pm. Upmarket place in a quiet street, close to Plaza Zocódover, with a tasty *menú* at €18. Regional specialities and game are on offer.

La Perdiz

C/Reyes Católicos 7. Daily 1–4pm & 8.30–midnight. Quality restaurant that does a very good *menú de degustación* for €21 and has a good selection of local wines too.

Restaurante Adolfo

C/Granada 6. Daily 1–4pm & 8.30–midnight. Closed Sun eve. Tucked behind a marzipan café, in an old Jewish town house, this is one of the best restaurants in town. It serves very imaginative takes on traditional Castilian food plus great desserts, all for around €35 a head. Be sure to ask to see the beautiful painted ceiling downstairs as well.

Restaurante Los Cuatro Tiempos

C/Sixto Ramón Parro 5. Daily 1–4pm & 8.30–midnight. Excellent mid-price restaurant with local specialities and good tapas, including delicious *caracoles* (snails). The *menu del día* is €18 and includes roast lamb.

Segovia

Strategically sited on a rocky ridge overlooking the Castilian plain, the small city of Segovia contains a panoply of architectural highlights that more than justify a visit. Most celebrated of its many treasures are the Roman aqueduct, the cathedral and the fairy-tale Alcázar, but it's also less obvious attractions – the ancient churches and mansions from the Golden Age when it was a royal resort and a base for the *cortes* (parliament) – that add to the city's appeal. Just a few kilometres east stands the Bourbon palace of La Granja, offering an alternative to Segovia's labyrinthine streets, with lavishly furnished rooms and beautifully tranquil gardens.

The Aqueduct

Plaza del Azoguejo. Over 800m long and at its highest point towering some 30m above the Plaza de Azoguejo, Segovia's aqueduct is an impressive sight. Built without a drop of mortar or cement, it has been here since around the end of the first century AD – no one knows exactly when – though it no longer carries water from the Río Frío to the city. In recent years traffic vibration and pollution have been threatening to undermine the entire structure, but the completion of a meticulous restoration programme should ensure it remains in place for some time to come.

For an excellent view of both the aqueduct and the city, climb the stairs beside it up to a surviving fragment of the city walls.

▼ SEGOVIA'S ROMAN AQUEDUCT

Arrival and information

Segovia is an easy day-trip from Madrid, with nine **trains** daily (1hr 50min–2hr) from Atocha and Charmartín stations, as well as up to 31 **buses**, operated by La Sepulvedana and leaving from Paseo de la Florida 11 (Metro Príncipe Pío; 1hr 45min). The city's own train station is some distance out of town – take bus #3 to the central Plaza Mayor; the bus station is on the same route.

There are **tourist offices** in the **Plaza Mayor** (daily 9am–8pm, Fri & Sat closes an hour later; ☏902 203 030, ⊛www.jcyl.es/turismo) and the busy **Plaza de Azoguejo** (daily 10am–8pm; ☏921 462 914) by the aqueduct; both provide maps and information.

There is a regular bus service from Segovia to La Granja operated by La Sepulvedana. It leaves from the bus station at Paseo Ezequiel González 12.

▲ THE CATHEDRAL

The Cathedral

Plaza Mayor. Daily: April–Oct
9am–6.30pm; Nov–March
9.30am–5.30pm. Free. Museum: same
hours as cathedral, except Sun opens
at 2.30pm. €1.80. Segovia's
cathedral was the last major
Gothic building constructed in
Spain, and arguably the last in
Europe. Pinnacles and flying
buttresses are tacked on at every
conceivable point, although the
interior is surprisingly bare and
its space is cramped by a great
green marble choir in the very
centre. The cathedral's treasures
– communion dishes, priestly
vestments and so on – are
almost all confined to the
museum, which is accessed from
the cloisters.

The Alcázar

Plaza Reina Victoria Eugenia. Daily:
April–Sept 10am–7pm; Oct–March
10am–6pm. €3, free Tues for EU
citizens. At the edge of town and
overlooking the valley of the
Río Eresma is the Alcázar, an
extraordinary fantasy of a castle.
With its narrow towers and
flurry of turrets, it seems eerily
familiar to just about every
visitor, having served as the
model for the original
Disneyland castle in California.

Although it dates from the
fourteenth and fifteenth
centuries, it was almost
completely destroyed by a fire in
1862 and rebuilt as a
deliberately exaggerated version
of the original. Inside, the rooms
are decked out with armour,
weapons and tapestries, but the
major attractions are the
splendid *artesonado* (wooden
sculptured) ceilings and the
magnificent panoramas from the
tower.

Synagogue-Church of Corpus Cristi

Plaza Corpus Cristi. Daily
9.30am–1.30pm & 4.30–6pm. One
of the lesser-known sights of
Segovia is its synagogue,
standing in a little courtyard
and now serving as the
convent church of Corpus
Cristi. It's very similar in style
to Santa María la Blanca in
Toledo (see p.147), though less
refined, and what you see
today is actually a
reconstruction as the original
was badly damaged by fire
during the nineteenth century.
Despite all this, it is still of
significant historic interest as
one of very few surviving
synagogue buildings in Spain.

EATING & DRINKING
Bar-Mesón Cuevas
de San Esteban   1
Mesón de Cándido   4
Mesón del Duque   3
Mesón José María   2

SEGOVIA   0   100m

Casa-Museo de Antonio Machado

C/Desamparados 5. Summer: Tues 11am–2pm, Wed–Sun 11am–2pm & 4.30–7.30pm; winter: Tues 11am–2pm, Wed–Sun 11am–2pm & 4–6pm. €1.50, free Wed. This little house displays the spartan accommodation and furnishings of one of Spain's greatest poets of the early twentieth century, Antonio Machado. Though generally associated with the town of Soria, Machado spent the last years of his life teaching here and this museum gives an interesting insight into life during that time.

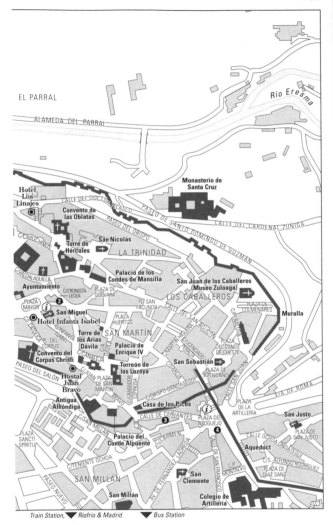

Train Station, ▼ Riofrio & Madrid   ▼ Bus Station

Museo de Brujería

C/Daoiz. Daily: summer
10.30am–2.30pm & 4.30–8.30pm;
winter 10.30am–2pm & 4–6.30pm.
€4. The Museum of Witchcraft
is of passing interest for most
visitors but a compulsory stop
for devotees of the dark arts.
Some three hundred ghoulish
exhibits related to the history of
witchcraft and related practices
brought together by an Italian
collector are on display in this
suitably atmospheric house.

Vera Cruz

Carretera Zamarramala. Tues–Sun:
summer 10.30am–1.30pm &

3.30–7pm; winter 10.30am–1.30pm & 3.30–6pm; closed Nov. €1.50. This remarkable twelve-sided church stands in the valley facing the Alcázar, and is reached by taking one of the paths that descend from the north side of the city walls. Built by the Knights Templar in the early thirteenth century on the pattern of the Church of the Holy Sepulchre in Jerusalem, it once housed part of the supposed True Cross (hence its name). Today, you can climb the tower for a highly photogenic view of the city, while nearby is a very pleasant riverside walk along the banks of the tranquil Río Eresma.

Convento de San Antonio Real

C/San Antonio Real. Tues–Sat 10am–2.30pm & 4–7.30pm, Sun 11am–2pm. €2. If you follow the line of the aqueduct away from the old city for about ten minutes, you will come to a little gem of a palace originally founded by Enrique IV in 1455 and containing an intriguing collection of Mudéjar and Hispano-Flemish art. The convent has some of the most beautiful *artesonado* (wooden sculptured) ceilings in the city and there's a wonderfully detailed fifteenth-century wooden Calvary in the main church.

La Granja

ⓦwww.patrimonionacional.es. Palace April–Sept Tues–Sun 10am–6pm; Oct–March Tues–Sat 10am–1.30pm & 3–5pm, Sun 10am–2pm. Compulsory guided tour €5, free Wed for EU citizens. Gardens daily: summer 10am–9pm; winter 10am–6pm. €3.40, free Wed for EU citizens. The summer palace of La Granja was built by the first Bourbon king of Spain, Felipe V, no doubt in another attempt to alleviate his homesickness for Versailles. Its chief appeal lies in its mountain

▲ SEGOVIA'S ALCÁZAR

▲ LA GRANJA FOUNTAIN

setting and extravagant wooded grounds and gardens, but it's also worth casting an eye over the palace which, though damaged by a fire in 1918, has been successfully restored. The rooms seen on the tour are furnished in plush French Imperial style and the palace is also home to one of the most valuable collections of sixteenth-century tapestries in the world.

Outside, the highlight of the eighteenth-century gardens is a series of majestic fountains. They're a fantastic spectacle, with some of the jets rising forty metres, but usually only operate at 5.30pm at weekends and on Wednesdays, with special displays on May 30, July 25 and August 25.

Restaurants

Bar-Mesón Cuevas de San Esteban

C/Valdelaguila 15, off the top end of Plaza San Esteban. Popular with the locals, this cavern-like restaurant and bar serves up excellent-value tapas and Castilian staples. The *menú del día* is €9.81.

Mesón de Cándido

Plaza Azoguejo 5 ☎921 428 103. In the shadow of the aqueduct stands the city's most famous restaurant, looked after by the original founder's son and still the place for *cochinillo* (suckling pig) and other roasts. Expect to pay €27 for the *cochinillo*.

Mesón del Duque

C/Cervantes 12 ☎921 462 487. Rival to the nearby *Cándido*, this place also specializes in Castilian roasts. The €25.50 *menú* includes *cochinillo*.

▲ SUCKLING PIG

Mesón José María

C/Cronista Lecea 11, just off Plaza Mayor ☎921 461 111. The city's best and most interesting restaurant, with modern variations on Castilian classics. The *menú* is a fairly steep €25, but individual dishes cost around €12.

Accommodation

Hotels and hostales

Madrid has a number of exclusive top-class hotels and plenty of comfortable but more functional options. *Hostales* are often a good alternative, offering small, frequently family-run establishments, sometimes with shared bathrooms, housed in large, centrally located apartment blocks.

The main factor to consider in choosing a place is location. To be at the heart of the old town, choose the areas around Puerta del Sol, Plaza de Santa Ana or Plaza Mayor; for nightlife, Malasaña or Chueca will appeal; if you want a quieter location and a bit more luxury, consider the Paseo del Prado, Recoletos or Salamanca areas. Another thing to bear in mind is noise. Madrid is a high-decibel city so avoid rooms on lower floors or choose a place away from the action. As for facilities, air conditioning is a welcome extra in summer.

Prices given in our reviews are for the cheapest double room available. Note that hotels add a seven-percent IVA (VAT) charge to the rates given below; for *hostales* the tax is already included.

Madrid de los Austrias

Hostal La Macarena C/Cava de San Miguel 8, 2° ☎913 659 221, ☎913 642 757. Decent, refurbished, family-run *hostal* in a characterful alley near Plaza Mayor. The well-kept rooms are on the small side, but all have bathroom, satellite TV and ceiling fans. Can be a little noisy, but the location is perfect. €65.

Hostal La Perla Asturiana Plaza de Santa Cruz 3 ☎913 664 600, ⊛www.perlaasturiana.com. Small, basic rooms in nicely located hostal that gives the sensation it was once a higher-class establishment. €47.

Hostal Rifer C/Mayor 5, 4° ☎915 323 197. Spotless, bright rooms, all with en-suite facilities, in the highest – and therefore quietest – of three options in this block. The friendly owner is anxious to please and has plans to upgrade the rooms. €42.

Booking accommodation

Madrid's increasing popularity as a weekend-break destination means that it's best to book accommodation in advance. Phoning or emailing is recommended; most places will understand English. It's also advisable to reconfirm the booking a few days in advance.

Hotels in the more expensive categories offer special weekend offers, so it's always worth checking their websites for details. If your Spanish is decent then the bancotel vouchers scheme is a great way of making huge savings on standard rates – they're available online at ⊛www.bancotel.es or at travel agents (see p.176).

If you do arrive without a reservation, accommodation services at the airport, the Estación Sur de Autobuses, and Atocha and Chamartín train stations can be useful. Brújula is particularly helpful, with offices at Atocha station (open daily 8am–10pm; ☎915 391 173) and Charmartín (daily 7.30am–9.30pm; ☎913 257 894). The service covers the whole of Spain and there's a €2.50 booking fee.

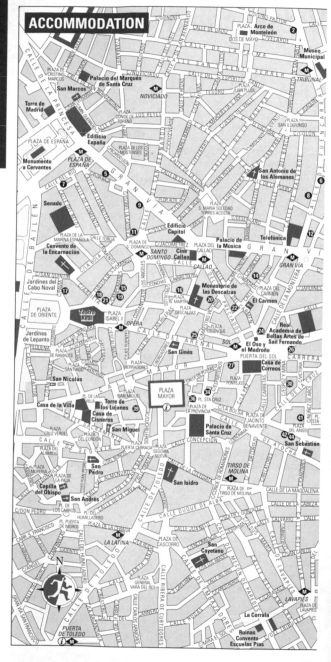

ACCOMMODATION

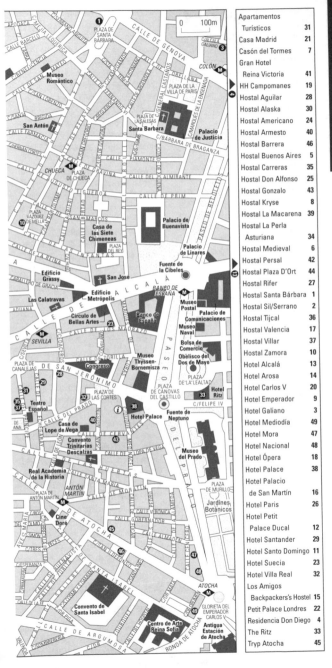

ACCOMMODATION

Apartamentos Turísticos	31
Casa Madrid	21
Casón del Tormes	7
Gran Hotel Reina Victoria	41
HH Campomanes	19
Hostal Aguilar	28
Hostal Alaska	30
Hostal Americano	24
Hostal Armesto	40
Hostal Barrera	46
Hostal Buenos Aires	5
Hostal Carreras	35
Hostal Don Alfonso	25
Hostal Gonzalo	43
Hostal Kryse	8
Hostal La Macarena	39
Hostal La Perla Asturiana	34
Hostal Medieval	6
Hostal Persal	42
Hostal Plaza D'Ort	44
Hostal Rifer	27
Hostal Santa Bárbara	1
Hostal Sil/Serrano	2
Hostal Tijcal	36
Hostal Valencia	17
Hostal Villar	37
Hostal Zamora	10
Hotel Alcalá	13
Hotel Arosa	14
Hotel Carlos V	20
Hotel Emperador	9
Hotel Galiano	3
Hotel Mediodía	49
Hotel Mora	47
Hotel Nacional	48
Hotel Ópera	18
Hotel Palace	38
Hotel Palacio de San Martín	16
Hotel Paris	26
Hotel Petit Palace Ducal	12
Hotel Santander	29
Hotel Santo Domingo	11
Hotel Suecia	23
Hotel Villa Real	32
Los Amigos Backpackers's Hostel	15
Petit Palace Londres	22
Residencia Don Diego	4
The Ritz	33
Tryp Atocha	45

Ópera

Los Amigos Backpackers' Hostel C/Campomanes 6, 4° izda ☎ & ☎915 471 707, ⊛www.losamigoshostel.com. Great backpacking option in a quiet side street, five minutes from Sol. Dormitories cater for 4–6 people, and there are a couple of communal rooms, plus access to the Internet. The friendly staff speak English, and bed linen and use of kitchen are included in the €16 price. Doubles for €37.50.

HH Campomanes C/Campomanes 4 ☎915 488 548, ⊛www.hhcampomanes .com. Chic designer hotel with a perfect location close to the Teatro Real. Staff are friendly and the rooms, though compact, have slick decor and cool bathrooms. Buffet breakfast included in the €99 price.

Hotel Carlos V C/Maestro Vitoria 5 ☎915 314 100, ⊛www.hotelcarlosv.com. Large hotel, behind the Descalzas Reales monastery. Some of the air-conditioned rooms on the fifth floor have balconies (at extra cost), though there isn't much of a view. There's an elegant lounge and café, and the hotel has a deal with a nearby car park which guests can use at reduced rates. Price includes breakfast. €94–124.

Casa Madrid C/Arrieta 2, 2° ☎915 595 791, ⊛www.casademadrid.com. Exclusive boutique-style hotel, offering seven stunning rooms decorated with hand-painted frescoes, classical statues, original paintings and fresh flowers. Ideal for a romantic escape, but not really the place for children. Doubles start at €195, while the suite is €350.

Hostal Don Alfonso Plaza Celenque 1, 2° ☎915 319 840, ☎915 329 225. This clean *hostal* is in a good location and has fourteen doubles, two triples and a handful of singles at a competitive price, all with bathrooms and TV. €48.

Hotel Ópera C/Cuesta de Santo Domingo 2 ☎915 412 800, ⊛www.hotelopera .com. This recently refurbished hotel has 79 large and comfortable rooms, all with free high-speed Internet connection. In keeping with the name, the waiters in the restaurant entertain diners with arias from operas and *zarzuelas*. €100.

Hotel Palacio de San Martín C/Plaza de San Martín 5 ☎917 015 000, ⊛www.intur.com/palacio.htm. This former US embassy building is now an elegant hotel offering 94 modern rooms, a small gym and sauna, plus a fine rooftop restaurant. Normal price is €204, but weekend offers go as low as €109.

Hostal Valencia Plaza de Oriente 23 ☎915 598 450. Fabulous location with great views over the plaza towards the Palacio Real. The seven quiet, old-style rooms are very clean and the owner is charming. €60.

The Rastro, Lavapíes and Embajadores

Hostal Barrera C/Atocha 96, 2A ☎915 275 381, ⊛www.hostalbarrera.com. Upmarket, friendly and good-value 14-room *hostal*, with an English-speaking owner. The rooms are a cut above most found in this category, the bathrooms have recently been re-equipped and air conditioning installed. One of the best in this part of town. €50.

Tryp Atocha C/Atocha 83 ☎913 300 500, ⊛www.trypatocha.solmelia.com. This large, business-style hotel has 150 modern rooms with all the facilities you'd expect. The usual price for a standard double is around €110, but special offers can bring it down to €88.

Sol, Santa Ana and Huertas

Hostal Aguilar Carrera de San Jerónimo 32, 2° ☎914 295 926 or 914 293 661, ⊛www.hostalaguilar.com. Large *hostal* offering airy rooms all with bath, TV and air conditioning. Guests also have access to the Internet. It specializes in multi-bed rooms offering very good prices for quad-ruples (€76), making an ideal budget place for families. Doubles are €47.

Hostal Alaska C/Espoz y Mina 7, 4° dcha ☎915 211 845, ⌨www.hostalalaska.com. Four doubles, a triple and a single in this friendly *hostal*, a stone's throw from Sol. All seven of the brightly decorated rooms have bathrooms and TV, and the owner, who speaks English, will go out of his way to make you feel at home. Doubles €40.

Hostal Americano Puerta del Sol 11, 3° & 4° ☎915 222 822, ⌨915 221 192. Nicely furnished 44-room *hostal* with recently improved bathrooms and a pleasant communal living room with great views over the bustling Puerta del Sol. €42.

Apartamentos Turísticos C/Príncipe 11 ☎902 113 311, ⌨www.atprincipe11.com. A good option for families or groups. The 36 apartments in this centrally located block range from small studios to family suites for up to six, all air-conditioned and with kitchenettes. Prices range from €96 for a four-person to €143 for a family one.

Hostal Armesto C/San Agustín 6, 1° dcha ☎914 290 940 or 914 299 031. A standard six-room *hostal*. All rooms have small bathrooms and TV and the best ones overlook the delightful little garden in the Casa de Lope de Vega next door. Very well positioned for the Huertas/Santa Ana area. €40.

Hostal Carreras c/Príncipe 18, 3° izqda ☎ & ⌨915 220 036. Large, light rooms in this very pleasant *hostal* located close to Plaza Santa Ana. Some of the 14 rooms have handbasins only and cost €36, others have showers or baths and are €48.

Hotel Paris c/Alcalá 2 ☎915 216 496, ⌨915 310 188. Old-fashioned and rather kitsch, the *Paris* was once one of the city's top hotels. It's no longer that, but is still a good option given its excellent location and the fact that half the spacious rooms have air conditioning. The €93 price includes breakfast.

Hostal Persal Plaza del Angel 12 ☎913

694 643, ⌨www.hostalpersal.com. Eighty-room *hostal* that is closer to a hotel in terms of services and facilities. All the rooms have air conditioning, bathrooms and TV, and are surprisingly quiet given the central location. Breakfast included. Doubles are €65–75 depending on the time of year.

Petit Palace Londres C/Galdo 2 ☎915 314 105, ⌨www.hthotels.com. One of a chain of smart high-tech hotels that offer very good rates and services. This one is in a refurbished mansion and has chic, well-equipped rooms with a range of facilities. Standard doubles are €125–130, but special offers can bring that down to €90–100 in August. The excellent buffet breakfast costs €10.

Hostal Plaza D'Ort Plaza del Angel 13, 1° ☎914 299 041, ⌨www.plazadort.com. All the smallish rooms in this very clean *hostal* have a shower or bath, TV, telephone and Internet connection, and some have air conditioning too. There are also several self-catering apartments, sleeping four to eight people for between €120–160 a night. Standard doubles cost €48.

Gran Hotel Reina Victoria Plaza de Santa Ana 14 ☎915 314 500, ⌨www.tryp reinavictoria.solmelia.com. The architecturally overblown *Reina Victoria* is a favourite of bullfighters, and has a taurine-themed bar, a rather grand foyer and all the services you'd expect, including currency exchange and a car park. Standard price is a hefty €217 a night, but frequent offers bring it down to nearer €100.

Hotel Santander C/Echegaray 1 ☎914 296 644, ⌨913 691 078. Perfectly located for the bars and restaurants in the Santa Ana/Huertas area, this hotel has spacious and spotless rooms with large bathrooms and classy old-fashioned decor, plus very friendly staff. Good value at €65 for a double.

Hotel Suecia C/Marqués de Casa Riera 4 ☎915 316 900, ⌨www.hotelsuecia.com. Tucked away behind the Círculo de Bellas Artes, the recently refurbished *Suecia* is a cut above the other options in this price range, with brightly decorated rooms and slick, professional service. Two completely non-smoking floors available. €142.

Hostal Tijcal C/Zaragoza 6, 3° ☎913 655 910, ⌨www.hostaltijcal.com. Quirky but extremely friendly *hostal* offering salmon pink rooms (some have good views) with bathroom, TV, very comfortable beds and air conditioning (€5 supplement). Triples and quadruples also available. A sister *hostal*, *Tijcal 2*, is at c/Cruz 26 ☎913 604 628, ☎915 211 477. €56–60 (cheaper if you pay in cash).

Hostal Villar C/Príncipe 18, 1° ☎915 316 600, ☎www.villar.arrakis.es. Large 46-room *hostal* spread over four floors, close to Sol and perfectly located for the Santa Ana/Huertas zone. The simple, clean rooms all have TVs and safes. Doubles with shared facilities €31.

The Paseo del Arte and the Retiro

Hostal Gonzalo C/Cervantes 34, 3° ☎914 292 714, ☎914 202 007. One of the most welcoming *hostales* in the city, tucked away close to Paseo del Prado. Twelve bright, en-suite rooms with TV and a fan. The charming owner, Antonio, and his brother Javier run a very smart place at an excellent price. Highly recommended. €50.

Hotel Mediodía Plaza del Emperador Carlos V 8 ☎915 273 060, ☎915 307 008. Huge, slightly faded 165-room hotel, next to the Reina Sofía and Atocha Station. The simple but comfortable rooms, all with bathroom and TV, are excellent value. Directly below, *El Brillante* café does a nice cup of coffee and some decent tapas. €69.

Hotel Mora Paseo del Prado 32 ☎914 201 569, ☎914 200 564. Friendly, recently refurbished 62-room hotel. All rooms have air conditioning and some have pleasant views along the Paseo del Prado (double glazing blocks out the worst of the traffic noise). Perfectly positioned for all the galleries and very good value too. €70.

Hotel Nacional Paseo del Prado 48 ☎914 296 629, ☎www.nh-hotels.com. Part of the high-quality *NH* chain, this large, plush hotel is attractively situated opposite the botanic gardens, and not that pricey, given the excellent facilities and luxurious surroundings. Standard price is €205 but weekend offers bring it down to as little as €85.

Hotel Palace Plaza de las Cortes 7 ☎913 608 000, ☎www.palacemadrid .com. Colossal, sumptuous hotel with every imaginable facility but none of the snootiness of the *Ritz* across the road. A spectacular, glass-covered central patio and luxurious rooms are part of its charm. Full-priced doubles are €439, but can drop to €199 with special offers.

The Ritz Plaza de la Lealtad 5 ☎917 016 767, ☎www.ritzmadrid.com. As opulent as you'd expect and popular with celebrities who can obviously bear the pretentious staff. If you want a quick peep, have an early evening cocktail in the leafy garden. The standard rate for a double is a wallet-busting €480, but deals can bring it down to half that.

Hotel Villa Real Plaza de las Cortes 10 ☎914 203 767, ☎www.derbyhotels.es. Classy and very original hotel, complete with its own art collection. Each of the 96 elegant double rooms has a spacious sitting area and the quality rooftop restaurant has fine views towards the Paseo del Prado. Full price is €337, but there are regular special offers for around €150.

Gran Vía, Chueca and Malasaña

Hotel Arosa C/Salud 21 ☎915 321 600, ☎www.bestwestern.com/es/arosa. Right in the heart of town, the spacious, air-conditioned rooms in this friendly, well-equipped hotel all have modern bathrooms and a safe. Some of the surrounding streets are a little down-at-heel, but don't let this put you off. Best rate options are €86, otherwise around €155 for a double.

Hostal Kryse C/Fuencarral 25, 1° izqda ☎915 311 512 or 915 228 153, ☎915 228 153. Welcoming 25-room *hostal* where all rooms have verandas, small bathrooms, TV, telephone and ceiling fans. One of a trio of places all run by the same management. €48.

Hostal Medieval C/Fuencarral 46, 2° ☎915 222 549. Well-run, friendly place in an old building overlooking a square. The range of airy rooms all have showers, but toilets are shared. €35.

Hotel Petit Palace Ducal C/Hortaleza 3, ☎915 211 043, ✆www.hthoteles.com. A major upgrade of a former *hostal*, this is part of a new chain of high-tech hotels in which all rooms have high-speed Internet connections and other mod cons. Stylish doubles cost €95.

Hostal Santa Bárbara Plaza Santa Bárbara 4 ☎914 457 334, ✆914 462 345. Rather upmarket *hostal* in a good location on a pleasant tree-lined square. The tidy little rooms – some with air conditioning – all have bathrooms and there's a great Art Deco TV salon too. English spoken. €62.

Hostal Sil/Serrano C/Fuencarral 95, 2º & 3º ☎914 488 972, ✆914 474 829. Two *hostales* run by a friendly owner at the quieter end of c/Fuencarral. A variety of rooms, all with air conditioning, newish bathrooms and TV, cost from €59.

Hostal Zamora Plaza Vázquez de Mella 1, 4º izqda ☎915 217 031. Seventeen simple rooms in an agreeable family-run place, most of which overlook the plaza. Some rooms have air conditioning, and all have modern bathrooms and TV. If you can't get in here, there are three other similar *hostales* in the same block. €42.

Salamanca

Hotel Alcalá C/Alcalá 66 ☎914 351 060, ✆www.nh-hotels.com. Large, classy hotel belonging to the efficient *NH* chain, just to the north of the Retiro, with smart rooms, professional staff, laundry facilities and a car park. Expensive, but good deals available during the summer and at weekends. Standard price €224, but special offers from €87.

Hotel Galiano C/Alcalá Galiano 6 ☎913 192 000, ✆www.hotelgaliano.com. Hidden away in a quiet street, this small hotel has a sophisticated air. There's a pleasant, well-furnished salon off the entrance lobby, staff are polite and the excellent rooms are air-conditioned. Breakfast costs €6. Car parking available. €120.

Residencia Don Diego C/Velázquez 45, 5º ☎914 350 760, ✆www .hostaldondiego.com. Comfortable, friendly, medium-sized hotel in an upmarket area of town. The quiet rooms, with full facilities, newly equipped bathrooms, air conditioning and satellite TV, are reasonably priced for the area. Some English-speaking staff. €87.

Plaza de España

Hotel Buenos Aires Gran Vía 61, 2º ☎915 420 102 or 915 422 250, ✆www.hoteleshn.com. A former hostal recently upgraded to a thirty-room hotel, whose pleasantly decorated rooms have air conditioning, satellite TV and modern bathrooms, plus double glazing to keep out much of the noise. €59.

Casón del Tormes C/Río 7 ☎915 419 746, ✆www.hotelcasondeltormes.com. Welcoming three-star place in a surprisingly quiet street. The 63 air-conditioned, ensuite rooms are very comfortable and hotel facilities include a bar and breakfast room, and helpful, English-speaking staff. €63 in July & Aug, €97 otherwise.

Hotel Emperador Gran Vía 53 ☎915 472 800, ✆www.emperadorhotel.com. The only real reason to come here is the superb rooftop swimming pool with its magnificent views, while the hotel itself is geared up for the organized tour market and is rather impersonal. The rooms are large and well decorated though. €140.

Hotel Santo Domingo Plaza Santo Domingo ☎915 479 800, ✆www.hotel-santodomingo.net. Modern, attractively decorated rooms in this well run and friendly hotel. Some of the more expensive ones have small terraces; all have air conditioning, satellite TV, minibars and a safe. €101 with reductions at the weekend.

Toledo

See map, p.144.

Hostal Descalzos C/Descalzos 30 ☎925 227 114, ✆www.hostaldescalzos.com. Very good-value, centrally located *hostal*, handy for the main sights. Some of the air-conditioned en-suite rooms have nice views, plus there's a small open-air pool too. €48–56.

Hotel Pintor el Greco C/Alamillos de Transito 13 ☎925 285 191, ⊛www.hotelpintorelgreco.com. Well-equipped and nicely furnished hotel in a refurbished seventeenth-century bakery in the old Jewish quarter. Many of the 33 rooms have fine views across the Rió Tajo. €102.

Hotel Santa Isabel C/Santa Isabel 24 ☎925 253 120, ⊛www.santa-isabel .com. Best of the mid-range hotels, housed in a converted nobleman's house right in the centre, with airy rooms, wood-panelled floors and safe parking. €42.

Segovia

See map, p.152.

Hotel Infanta Isabel Plaza Mayor 12 ☎921 461 300, ⊛www.hotelinfantais-abel.com. Comfortable new hotel with air-conditioned rooms, housed in a renovated nineteenth-century building. €74.

Hostal Juan Bravo C/Juan Bravo 12 ☎921 463 413. This good budget option has comfortable rooms and plant-festooned bathrooms. €34.

Hotel Los Linajes C/Dr Velasco 9 ☎921 460 475, ⊛hotelloslinajes@terra.es. Good-value cosy hotel, set in part of an old palace. It has a fine garden overlooking the river valley, and all rooms are air-conditioned. Own parking too. €79.

Essentials

Arrival

Whatever your point of arrival, it's easy to get into the centre of Madrid. The airport is connected by metro, shuttle buses and taxis, while the city's main train and bus stations are linked to the metro system.

By air

The **Aeropuerto de Barajas** (general information ☎913 936 000, flight information ☎902 353 570, ⊛www.aena.es) is 16km east of the city. It has three interconnecting terminals: T1 for nearly all international flights (*vuelos internacionales*); T2 for domestic flights (*nacionales*) plus some of Iberia's flights from continental Europe; and T3 for the Puente Aéreo (the air shuttle with Barcelona). A vast new Richard Rogers–designed terminal building is scheduled to open in 2005 and will double the present capacity.

From the airport, the **metro** link (Line 8) takes you from T2 to the city's Nuevos Ministerios station – where check-in facilities for some airlines are available for your return journey – in just twelve minutes (daily 6am–1.30am, Fri & Sat until 2.30am; €1.15). From there, connecting metro lines make most city-centre locations just a fifteen-minute ride away.

There's a **shuttle bus** that departs from outside each terminal every ten to fifteen minutes (daily 4.45am–2am; €2.50) running to an underground terminal in the central Plaza Colón (Metro Serrano; pedestrian entrance on c/Goya), taking from twenty minutes to an hour depending on traffic. If your plane arrives outside these times, there should be additional connecting bus services. **Taxis** are always available outside and cost €18–20 to the centre.

By land

Trains from France and northern Spain arrive at the **Estación de Chamartín**, a modern terminal in the far north of the city, connected by metro with the centre, and by regular commuter trains (*trenes de cercanías*) to the much more central **Estación de Atocha**. Atocha has two separate terminals: one for **Toledo** and other local services; the other for all points in **southern and eastern Spain**, including the high-speed AVE services. For train **information and reservations** call ☎ 902 240 202 or go to ⊛www .renfe.es.

Bus terminals are scattered throughout the city, but the largest – used by all of the international bus services – is the **Estación Sur de Autobuses** on c/Méndez Álvaro, 1.5km south of Atocha train station (☎914 684 200, ⊛www.estaciondeautobuses .com; Metro Méndez Álvaro).

Arriving **by car**, all main roads into Madrid bring you right into the city centre, although eccentric signposting and even more eccentric driving can be unnerving. The inner ring road, the M-30, and the Paseo de la Castellana, the main north–south artery, are both notorious bottlenecks, although virtually the whole city centre can be close to gridlock during **rush-hour periods** (Mon–Fri 7.30–9.30am & 6–8.30pm). Be prepared for a long trawl around the streets to find **parking** and even when you find somewhere, in most central areas you'll have to buy a ticket at one of the roadside metres (€1.50 for a maximum of two hours in the blue-coloured bays; €1.20 for a maximum of one hour in the green-coloured bays). Another option is to put your car in one of the many signposted *parkings* (€1.65 for the first hour, then €1.45 for subsequent hours). Once in the city, and with public transport being both efficient and good value, your own vehicle is really only of use for out-of-town excursions.

Information

There are year-round **turismo offices** at several points across the city (see below for details), supplemented in the summer by turismo posts at popular spots such as the Puerta del Sol and the Prado. There are also **visitor helpers**, in blue and yellow uniforms, outside the Palacio Real, Plaza de la Villa and the Prado, and in the Plaza Mayor, Puerta del Sol, Plaza del Callao and the Estación Sur de Autobuses. They speak English and can provide information about all the major sights and tourist services. The Madrid tourist board's website (ⓦwww.munimadrid.es /turismo) has details on accommodation and eating out, as well as tours and events; the regional authority's site (ⓦwww.madrid.org/turismo) has similar information, covering the whole of Madrid province. You can **phone for tourist information** in English on ☎902 100 007, a premium rate number that links all the regional turismo offices mentioned below.

Listings information is in plentiful supply in Madrid. The **newspapers** *El País* (ⓦwww.elpais.es) and *El Mundo* (ⓦwww.metropoli.com) have excellent daily listings (in Spanish), and on Friday both publish sections devoted to events, bars and restaurants in the capital. If your time in Madrid doesn't coincide with the Friday supplements, or you want a full rundown, pick up the weekly **listings magazine** *La Guía del Ocio* (ⓦwww .guiadelocio.com; €1) at any newsagent's stand. The *ayuntamiento* (city council) also publishes a monthly what's-on pamphlet, *En Madrid* (in English and Spanish), free from any of the tourist offices. Finally, *In Madrid* (ⓦwww.in-madrid.com) is a free monthly magazine, available in bars, that features useful reviews of nightlife.

For getting around, the **maps** in this book should be enough for navigating the centre, or there's the *Rough Guide City Map Madrid* that pinpoints sights, hotels, restaurants and bars. Free maps of the city are also available from any of the turismos.

Tourist offices

Barajas International Airport Mon–Fri 8am–8pm, Sat & Sun 8am–2pm. ☎913 058 656.

Estación de Atocha Mon–Fri 9am–9pm, Sat & Sun 9am–1pm. ☎902 100 007. Metro Atocha Renfe.

Estación de Chamartín Mon–Fri 8am–8pm, Sat 9am–2pm. ☎913 159 976. Metro Chamartín.

Plaza Mayor Mon–Sat 10am–8pm, Sun 10am–3pm. ☎915 881 636. Metro Sol.

Mercado Puerta de Toledo Ronda de Toledo 1. Mon–Fri 9am–7pm, Sat 9.30am–2.30pm. ☎913 641 876. Metro Puerta de Toledo.

C/Duque de Medinaceli 2 Mon–Fri 9am–7pm, Sat 9am–3pm. ☎914 294 951. Metro Banco de España.

The Madrid card

The **Madrid tourist card** (ⓦwww.madridcard.com) gives the holder free use of public transport, admission to 40 major museums, an open-top bus tour and a guided walk of the old city, plus discounts at a number of shops and restaurants. It costs €28 for one day (€42 for two, €55 for three) and is on sale at the Plaza Mayor, Atocha Station and c/Duque de Medinaceli tourist offices, as well as in International Arrivals at the airport. Do your sums before you splash out though, as you need to cram a lot into a day's sightseeing to get your money's worth.

City transport

Madrid is an easy city to get around. The central areas are walkable, the metro is modern and efficient, buses serve out-of-the-way districts, and taxis are always available.

If you're using public transport extensively and staying long-term, **passes** (*abonos*) covering the metro, train and bus, and available for each calendar month, are worthwhile. The standard ticket covering all the metro and buses in the city costs €34.55 and is available at *estancos* (tobacconists and stamp shops identified by a yellow and brown sign) and metro stations.

The metro

The clean and reliable **metro** (ⓦwww.metromadrid.es) is by far the quickest way of getting around Madrid, serving most places you're likely to want to get to. It runs from 6am until 2am (Fri & Sat until 2.30am) and the flat fare is €1.15, or €5.35 for a ten-trip ticket (*bono de diez viajes*), which can be used on buses too. Lines are numbered and colour-coded, and the direction of travel is indicated by the name of the terminus station. You can pick up a free colour map of the system (*plano del metro*) at any station.

Buses

The comprehensive **bus network** (ⓦwww.emtmadrid.es) is a good way to get around and see the sights. There are information booths at Plaza de Cibeles and Puerta del Sol, which dispense a huge route map (*plano de los transportes de Madrid*) and also sell bus passes. Fares are the same as the metro, at €1.15 a journey, or €5.35 for a ten-trip ticket (*bono de diez viajes*) which can be used on both forms of transport. When you get on the bus, punch your ticket in a machine by the driver. You can also buy tickets from the driver, but try and have the right money.

Services run from 6am to midnight, with *búho* (owl) buses operating through the night on twenty routes around the central area and out to the suburbs: departures are half-hourly midnight–5.30am from Plaza de Cibeles and Puerta del Sol, and the fare is the standard €1.15.

Taxis

Madrid has thousands of reasonably priced **taxis** that you can wave down on the street – look for white cars with a diagonal red stripe on the side. €6 will

---

Useful bus routes

#2 From west to east across town: from Argüelles metro station running along c/Princesa, past Plaza de España, along Gran Vía, past Cibeles and out past the Retiro.

#3 From south to north: Puerta de Toledo, through Sol, up towards Gran Vía and then Alonso Martínez and northwards.

#5 From Sol via Cibeles, Colón and the Paseo de la Castellana to Chamartín.

#27 From Embajadores, via Atocha, up the length of the Castellana to Plaza de Castilla.

#33 From Príncipe Pío out via the Puente de Segovia to the Parque de Atracciones and Zoo in Casa de Campo.

#C The Circular bus route takes a broad circuit round the city from Atocha, via Puerta de Toledo, Plaza de España, Moncloa, Cuatro Caminos, Avenida de América and Goya.

ESSENTIALS

Festivals and events

City tours

The turismo in Plaza Mayor (see p.170) can supply details of guided English-language **walking tours** around the city. A tour of Madrid de los Austrias departs at 10am on Saturdays from the Plaza Mayor tourist office and costs €6 (for more information on this and other walks see ⓦwww.munimadrid.es/turismo; info ☎915 882 906/7, reservations ☎902 221 622). For a **bus tour** of all the major sights try Madrid Vision (☎917 791 888, ⓦwww.madridvision.es); tickets cost €10.60 (children €5.30, under-7s free) and allow you to jump on and off at various points throughout the city. Pick-up points include Puerta del Sol, Plaza de España and the Prado.

get you most places within the centre and, although it's common to round up the fare, you're not expected to tip. The minimum fare is €1.55 and supplements (€2.20–4.20) are charged for baggage, going to the airport, train and bus stations or outside the city limits, and for night trips (11pm–7am). To phone for a taxi, call ☎915 478 200, 915 478 600 (also for wheelchair-friendly cabs), 914 051 213 or 914 459 008. If you want to make a complaint, take the driver's number and ask for the *hoja de reclamaciones* (a claim form).

Local trains

The **local train** network, or *cercanías*, is the most efficient way of connecting between the main railway stations and also provides the best route out to many of the suburbs and nearby towns. Most trains are air-conditioned, fares are cheap and there are good connections with the metro. Services generally run every fifteen to thirty minutes from 6am to midnight/1am. For more information go to the RENFE website at ⓦwww.renfe.es and click on the *cercanías* section for Madrid.

Festivals and events

In common with the rest of Spain, Madrid is not short of **festivals**, some involving the whole city, others just an individual barrio. The more important dates celebrated in the capital are listed below.

Also worth checking out are **cultural events** organized by the city council, in particular the Veranos de la Villa (July–Sept) and Festival de Otoño (Sept–Nov) concerts (classical, rock, flamenco), theatre and cinema. Many events are free and, in the summer, often open air, taking place in the city's parks and squares. Annual festivals for alternative theatre (Feb), flamenco (Feb), books (end of May), dance (April–May), photography (mid-June to mid-July) and jazz (Nov) are also firmly established on the cultural agenda. Information on all events can be found in the listings sources on p.170 and on the city's website ⓦwww.munimadrid.es.

January
Cabalgata de los Reyes (Cavalcade of the Three Kings) To celebrate the arrival of the gift-bearing Three Kings, January 5 sees a procession through the centre of Madrid in which children are showered with sweets. It's held on the evening before presents are traditionally exchanged in Spain.

February–April
Carnaval Held the week before Lent, this is the excuse for a lot of partying and fancy-dress parades, especially in the gay zone around Chueca. The end of *Carnaval* is marked by the bizarre and entertaining

parade, *El Entierro de la Sardina* (The Burial of the Sardine), on the Paseo de la Florida.

Semana Santa Easter week is celebrated with a series of solemn processions around Madrid, with Jueves Santo (Maundy Thursday) and Viernes Santo (Good Friday) both public holidays in Spain. Toledo also has very popular parades against the impressive backdrop of the city's ancient streets (routes and times of processions are available from tourist offices).

May

Fiesta del Dos de Mayo The May 2 celebrations around Madrid, but particularly in Malasaña, are held to commemorate the city's uprising against the French in 1808. Bands and partying take place around the main festive focus, Plaza Dos de Mayo.

Fiestas de San Isidro Madrid's patron saint's day, May 15, is marked with festivities – some of the biggest in the country – that actually spread over a week. The non-stop round of carnival events includes parades and loads of free entertainment, and usually centres on Plaza Mayor. Evenings generally start out with traditional *chotis* music and dancing, and there are also bands playing each night in the Jardines de las Vistillas (south of the Palacio Real). The fiestas also herald the start of the bullfighting season.

La Feria del Libro At the end of May, Madrid's great book fair takes place with hundreds of stands set up in the Retiro Park.

June–July

Gay Pride Week Usually celebrated at the end of June or beginning of July, Gay Pride is a week-long party throughout Chueca culminating in a massive carnival-style parade that brings the city centre to a standstill.

August

Castizo fiestas From August 6–15, authentic Madrileños put on lively, traditional *fiestas* to celebrate the saints' days of *San Cayetano*, *San Lorenzo* and *La Virgen de la Paloma*. Taking place across the areas of La Latina and Lavapiés, much of the activity centres around Calle Toledo, the Plaza de la Paja and the Jardines de las Vistillas.

December

Navidad The Christmas period in Madrid sees Plaza Mayor taken over by a model of a nativity crib and a large seasonal market with stalls selling all manner of festive decorations. El Corte Inglés department store, at the bottom of c/Preciados, has an all-singing-all-dancing clockwork Christmas scene that plays at regular intervals during the day to the delight of assembled children.

Noche Vieja New Year's Eve is celebrated at bars, restaurants and parties all over the city, and there are bands in some of the squares. Puerta del Sol is the customary place to gather for midnight, waiting for the strokes of the clock and then attempting to swallow a grape on each strike to bring good luck in the coming year.

Directory

ADDRESSES Calle (street) is abbreviated to c/ in addresses, followed by the number on the street, then another number that indicates the floor, eg c/Gijón 23, 5° means fifth floor of no. 23 Gijón Street. You may also see *izquierda* and *derecha*, meaning left or right (apartment or office) of the staircase.

AIRLINES Aer Lingus ☎915 414 216, ⊛www.aerlingus.ie; **Air Europa** ☎902 401 501, ⊛www.air-europa.com; **Air France** ☎901 112 266, ⊛www.airfrance.com; **American Airlines** ☎901 100 000, 914 531 400, ⊛www.aa.com; **British Airways**

☎902 111 333, ⊛www.britishairways.com; **British Midland** ⊛www.flybmi.com; easyJet ☎902 299 992, ⊛www.easyjet.com; **Iberia** ☎915 878 156, ⊛www.iberia.com; **KLM** ☎902 222 747, ⊛www. klm.com.

BANKS AND EXCHANGE Banks are plentiful throughout the city and are the best places to change money. **Opening hours** are normally Mon–Fri 9am–2pm, but some banks also open Sat 9am–1pm from October to May. Branches of El Corte Inglés have exchange offices with long hours and reasonably competitive rates; the most central is on c/Preciados, close to Puerta del Sol. Barajas Airport also has a 24-hour currency exchange office. The rates at the exchange bureaux scattered around the city are often very poor, though they don't usually charge commission.

ATM **cash machines** (cajeros automáticos) are widespread and accept most credit and debit cards. They're often the most convenient way to get cash, though it's wise to have a back-up source of funds. **Credit cards** are widely accepted in hotels, restaurants and shops.

CAR RENTAL Major operators have branches at the airport and train stations. Central offices include: **Atesa** Atocha ☏915 061 846, ✉www.atesa.com; **Avis** Gran Vía 60 ☏915 472 048, reservations ☏902 135 531, ✉www.avisworld.com; **Europcar** c/San Leonardo 8 ☏917 211 222, ✉www.europcar.com; **Hertz** Atocha Station ☏914 681 318, ✉www.hertz.com. **Easy-Rent-a-Car** c/Agustín de Foxa 27, Parking Centro Norte and Parking Garage Ruiz (1st floor), Ronda de Atocha 12 ☏0906 586 0586 (telephone bookings available from Britain only), ✉www.easycar.com.

CHILDREN Many of Madrid's main sights lack children-specific activities, but there's plenty to keep kids occupied during a short stay, from various parks – the Retiro being a particular favourite (see p.98) – to swimming pools (see p.175). Children are, in general, doted on in Spain and welcome in nearly all cafés and restaurants.

CINEMA Madrileños love going to the cinema (cine) and, though most foreign films are dubbed into Spanish, a number of cinemas have original-language screenings, listed in a separate versión original/subtitulada (v.o.) section in the newspapers. **Tickets** cost €5.50–5.75 but most cinemas have a día del espectador (usually Mon or Wed) with €4–4.25 admission. Be warned that on Sunday night half of Madrid goes to the movies and queues can be long. The most central cinemas showing v.o. films include the **Alphaville** and **Renoir** on c/Martín de los Heros, and **Princesa** on c/Princesa 3, all three next to Plaza de España, and the nine-screen **Ideal Yelmo Complex**, c/Doctor Cortezo 6, south off c/Atocha and near Plaza Santa Ana.

DISABLED TRAVELLERS Madrid is not particularly well geared up for disabled visitors (minusválidos), although the situation is gradually improving. The Organizacíon Nacional de Ciegos de España (ONCE; National Organisation for the Blind, c/Prado 24 ☏915 894 600, ✉www.once.es) provides specialist advice, as does the Federación de Asociaciones de Minusválidos Físicos de la Comunidad de Madrid (FAMMA, c/Galileo 69 ☏915 933 550, ✉www.famma.org). Wheelchair-accessible taxis can be ordered from Radio Taxi (☏915 478 200 or 915 478 600).

EMBASSIES Australia Plaza Descubridor Diego Ordás 3 ☏914 419 300, ✉www.embaustralia.es; **Britain** c/Fernando el Santo 16 ☏913 190 200, ✉www.ukinspain.com; **Canada** c/Núñez de Balboa 35 ☏914 314 300, ✉www.canada-es.org; **Ireland** Paseo de la Castellana 46 ☏913 190 200; **New Zealand** Plaza Lealtad 2 ☏915 230 226; **USA** c/Serrano 75 ☏915 774 000, ✉www.embusa.es.

EMERGENCIES For police, medical services and the fire brigade call ☏112.

GAY AND LESBIAN VISITORS The main gay organization in Madrid is Coordinadora Gay de Madrid, c/Fuencarral 37 (Mon–Fri 5–9pm, Aug from 7pm; ☏915 224 517, ✉www.cogam.org), which can give information on health, leisure and gay rights, and produces its own free monthly newsletter. For a good one-stop shop with lots of info on the gay scene, try Berkana Bookshop, c/Hortaleza 64 (Mon–Sat 10.30am–9pm; Sun noon–2pm & 5–9pm; ✉www.libreriaberkana.com).

HOSPITALS El Clínico Plaza de Cristo Rey ☏913 303 747; **Hospital Gregorio Marañon** c/Dr Esquerdo 46 ☏915 868 000; **Ciudad Sanitaria La Paz** Paseo de la Castellana 261 ☏913 582 831. First-aid stations are scattered throughout the city and open 24 hours a day: one of the most central is at c/Navas de Tolosa 10, just south of Plaza Callao (☏915 210 025). English-speaking doctors are available at the Anglo-American Medical Unit, c/Conde de Aranda 1 ☏914 351 823; Mon–Fri 9am–8pm, Sat 10am–3pm.

INTERNET ACCESS The best equipped and most central Internet cafés are the two run by Bbigg at c/Alcalá 21 and c/Mayor 1 (✉www.BBIGG.com), both of which are close to Puerta del Sol. Prices start at €1.20 per hour.

LEFT LUGGAGE There are left-luggage facilties (consignas) at Barajas Airport in terminals 1 and 2 (open 24 hours; €2.60 for up to 24 hours and €4.55 per day up to a maximum of 15), the Estación Sur and Conde de Casal bus stations, and lockers at Atocha (open 6.30am–10.20pm) and Chamartín (open 7am–11.30pm) train stations.

ENTRANCE FEES Madrid's clutch of top-notch museums, galleries and palaces often offer **free entrance** on certain days of the week. Sites classed as *Patrimonio Nacional* such as the Palacio Real, the Convento de la Encarnación, El Pardo and the Monasterio de las Descalzas are free to EU citizens on Wednesdays (bring your passport). Seven museums run by Madrid City Council including the Museo Municipal, the Museo de San Isidro, La Ermita de San Antonio and the Templo de Debod no longer charge admission at all. Most museums are free for under-18s and give substantial discounts to retired visitors and students (bring ID in all cases). In addition, many places that normally charge entry, set aside certain times when entrance is free (see our reviews for details) and nearly all of them throw their doors open on May 18, International Museum Day.

OPENING HOURS Spain in general, and Madrid in particular, operate on a different clock to much of Europe. Smaller shops generally open 10am–2pm and 5–8pm Monday to Friday, but only open in the mornings on Saturday. Department stores and chains tend not to close for lunch, open all day Saturday, and larger ones open on the first Sunday of the month too (except in August). Restaurants generally serve from 1.30pm to 4pm and 8.30pm to midnight, with many closing for a rest day on Monday. Bars stay open till the early hours – usually around 2am – while clubs and discobares can open until around 5am, depending on the licence they hold.

PHARMACIES *Farmacias* are distinguished by a green cross and can be found across the city. Each district has a pharmacy staying open through the night – for details check the notice on the door of your nearest one or call ☏098 (Spanish only).

POLICE If you've had something stolen, head to one of the following centrally located police stations (*comisarías*) to report the crime: c/Luna 29 (☏915 211 236; Metro Callao), c/Huertas 76 (☏912 490 994; Metro Antón Martín) or c/Leganitos 19 (☏915 417 160; Metro Santo Domingo). You will need to fill in an official report (*denuncia*) for insurance purposes which can be a time-consuming business. In an emergency call ☏112.

POST OFFICE The main post office is the Palacio de Comunicaciones on Plaza de las Cibeles (Mon–Sat 8.30am–9.30pm). The easiest places to buy stamps (*sellos*) are the *estancos*, recognizable by their brown and yellow signs bearing the word *Tabacos*.

PUBLIC HOLIDAYS The main national holidays when shops and banks close are: Jan 1 (Año Nuevo); Jan 6 (Reyes); Easter Thursday (Jueves Santo); Good Friday (Viernes Santo); May 1 (Fiesta del Trabajo); May 2 (Día de la Comunidad); May 15 (San Isidro); Aug 15 (Virgen de la Paloma); Oct 12 (Día de la Hispanidad); Nov 1 (Todos Los Santos); Nov 9 (Virgen de la Almudena); Dec 6 (Día de la Constitución); Dec 8 (La Inmaculada); Dec 25 (Navidad).

SWIMMING POOLS AND AQUAPARKS The Piscina Canal Isabel II, Avda de Filipinas 54 (daily 10am–8.30pm; Metro Ríos Rosas), is a large and well-maintained outdoor swimming pool and, the best central option. Alternatively, try the open-air *piscina* in the Casa de Campo (daily 10am–8.30pm; Metro El Lago). Both pools have café/bars attached. The rooftop pool of the *Hotel Emperador* (see p.165) on Gran Vía offers fantastic views across the city but is pricey for non-residents (June–Sept Mon–Thurs €25, Fri–Sun €35). There are also a number of **aquaparks** around the city, the closest being Aquamadrid, 16km out on the N-II Barcelona road (Bus Continental Auto #281, #282, #282, or #385 from Avda de América). Outside May–Sept most outdoor pools are closed.

TELEPHONES International calls can be made from any phone box or *locutorio* (call centre). The main *Telefónica* office at Gran Vía 30 has ranks of phones and is open until midnight. Phones accept either coins or phonecards that cost €5, €10, €15 and €20 from post offices or *estancos*. Calling Madrid from abroad, dial your international access code, then 34, followed by the subscriber's number which will nearly always start with 91. **Mobile phone users** from the UK should be able to use their phones in Spain – check with your service provider before leaving about costs. Most American cellphones do not work with the Spanish mobile network.

THEATRE As befits the nation's capital, Madrid has a vibrant theatre scene which, if you speak the language, is well worth sampling. You can catch anything from Lope de Vega to contemporary and experimental productions, and there is a particularly good range on offer during the annual *Festival de Otoño* which runs from September to November. For information on current productions, check the listings sources on p.170.

TICKET AGENCIES For theatre and concert tickets try: Tele-Entradas ☏902 150 025, ⊛www.bbvaticket.com; Caixa de Catalunya ☏902 101 212, ⊛www.caixacatalunya.es;

Caja de Madrid ☎902 488 488; El Corte Inglés ☎902 400 222, ✉www.elcorteingles.es; FNAC ☎915 956 100; Madrid Rock ☎915 236 652; and Servi-Caixa ☎902 332 211, ✉wwwlacaixa.es.

TIME Madrid is one hour ahead of Greenwich Mean Time so when it's noon in Madrid, it's 11am in London, 6am in New York, 3am in Los Angeles and 8pm in Sydney. Clocks go forward in late March and back an hour in late October.

TIPPING Tipping is not as important in Spain as it is, say, in the United States. Adding around five to ten percent to a restaurant bill is perfectly acceptable (more if the service was exceptional), while in bars and taxis, rounding up to the nearest euro is the norm.

TRAVEL AGENTS Víajes Zeppelin Plaza Santo Domingo 2 (☎915 477 904. Metro Santo Domingo), are English-speaking and very efficient. The popular high-street agencies **Halcón Viajes** (C/Goya 23) and **Viajes Marsans** (Gran Vía 63) have other branches across the city and are a good place to find hotel vouchers (see p.159). Many other travel agents are concentrated on and around Gran Vía and c/Princesa.

Language

Spanish

Once you get into it, Spanish is one of the easiest languages around, and people are eager to try and understand even the most faltering attempt. English is spoken at the main tourist attractions, but you'll get a far better reception if you try communicating with Madrileños in their own tongue.

Pronunciation

The rules of **pronunciation** are pretty straightforward and strictly observed.

A somewhere between the A sound of back and that of father.

E as in get.

I as in police.

O as in hot.

U as in rule.

C is spoken like a TH before E and I, hard otherwise: *cerca* is pronounced "thairka".

G is a guttural H sound (like the ch in loch) before E or I, a hard G elsewhere – *gigante* becomes "higante".

H is always silent.

J is the same as a guttural G: *jamón* is "hamon".

LL sounds like an English Y: *tortilla* is pronounced "torteeya".

N is as in English unless it has a tilde (accent) over it, when it becomes NY: *mañana* sounds like "manyana".

QU is pronounced like an English K.

R is rolled, RR doubly so.

V sounds more like B, *vino* becoming "beano".

X has an S sound before consonants, normal X before vowels.

Z is the same as a soft C, so *cerveza* becomes "thairbaytha".

Words and phrases

Basics

yes, no, ok	sí, no, vale
please, thank you	por favor, gracias
where?, when?	¿dónde?, ¿cuando?
what?, how much?	¿qué?, ¿cuánto?
here, there	aquí, allí
this, that	esto, eso
now, later	ahora, más tarde
open, closed	abierto/a, cerrado/a
with, without	con, sin
good, bad	buen(o)/a, mal(o)/a
big, small	gran(de), pequeño/a
cheap, expensive	barato, caro
hot, cold	caliente, frío
more, less	más, menos
today, tomorrow	hoy, mañana
yesterday	ayer
the bill	la cuenta
price	precio
free	gratis

Greetings and responses

hello, goodbye	hola, adiós
good morning	buenos días
good afternoon/ night	buenas tardes/noches

see you later	hasta luego
sorry	lo siento/disculpe
excuse me	con permiso/perdón
How are you?	¿Como está (usted)?
I (don't) understand	(no) entiendo
not at all/you're welcome	de nada
Do you speak english?	¿Habla (usted) inglés?
I (don't) speak Spanish	(no) hablo español
My name is . . .	Me llamo . . .
What's your name?	¿Como se llama usted?
I am English/ Scottish/Welsh/ Australian/ Canadian/ American/ Irish/ a New Zealander	Soy inglés(a)/ escocés(a)/galés(a)/ australiano(a)/ canadiense(a)/ americano(a)/ irlandés(a)/ neocelandés(a)

Hotels, transport and directions

I want	Quiero
I'd like	Quisiera
Do you know . . .?	¿Sabe . . .?
I don't know	No sé
there is (is there)?	(¿)hay(?)
Give me (one like that)	Deme (uno así)
Do you have . . .?	¿Tiene . . .?
the time	la hora
a room	una habitación
with two beds/ double bed	con dos camas/ cama matrimonial
with shower/bath	con ducha/baño
it's for one person	es para una persona
for one night	para una noche
for one week	para una semana
how do I get to . . .?	¿por donde se va a . . .?
left, right, straight on	izquierda, derecha, todo recto
Where is the bus station/post office/ toilet?	¿Dónde está la estación de autobuses/la oficina de correos/el baño?
What's this in spanish?	¿Cómo se llama esto en español?
Where does the bus to . . . leave from?	¿De dónde sale el autobús para . . .?
I'd like a (return) ticket to . . .	quisiera un billete (de ida y vuelta) para. . .
What time does it leave?	¿a qué hora sale?

Numbers and days

1	un/uno/una
2	dos
3	tres
4	cuatro
5	cinco
6	seis
7	siete
8	ocho
9	nueve
10	diez
11	once
12	doce
13	trece
14	catorce
15	quince
16	diez y seis
17	diez y siete
20	veinte
21	veintiuno
30	treinta
40	cuarenta
50	cincuenta
60	sesenta
70	setenta
80	ochenta
90	noventa
100	cien(to)
101	ciento uno
200	doscientos
500	quinientos
1000	mil

Monday	lunes
Tuesday	martes
Wednesday	miércoles
Thursday	jueves
Friday	viernes
Saturday	sábado
Sunday	domingo
today	hoy
yesterday	ayer
tomorrow	mañana

Food and drink

aceitunas	olives
agua	water
ahumados	smoked fish
al ajillo	with olive oil and garlic
a la marinera	seafood cooked with garlic, onions and white wine
a la parilla	charcoal-grilled
a la plancha	grilled on a hot plate
a la romana	fried in batter

albóndigas	meatballs
almejas	clams
anchoas	anchovies
anís	aniseed liqueur
arroz	rice
asado	roast
bacalao	cod
berenjena	aubergine/eggplant
bocadillo	french-loaf sandwich
boquerones	small, anchovy-like fish, usually served in vinegar
café (con leche)	(white) coffee
calamares	squid
callos	tripe
cangrejo	crab
caracoles	snails
carta	menu
cebolla	onion
cerveza	beer
champiñones	mushrooms
chorizo	spicy sausage
cochinillo	roast suckling pig
cocido	meat and chickpea stew
conejo	rabbit
croquetas	croquettes, usually with bits of ham in
cuchara	spoon
cuchillo	knife
empanada	slices of fish/meat pie
ensalada	salad
ensaladilla	Russian salad (diced vegetables in mayonnaise, often with tuna)
fresa	strawberry
gambas	prawns
hígado	liver
huevos (revueltos/fritos)	(scrambled/fried) eggs
jamón serrano	cured ham
jamón de york	regular ham
langostinos	langoustines
lechuga	lettuce
manzana	apple
mejillones	mussels
menú (del día)	daily set-lunch
menú de degustación	set menu offering a taste of several house specialities
morcilla	black pudding
naranja	orange
ostras	oysters
pan	bread
patatas alioli	potatoes in garlic mayonnaise
patatas bravas	fried potatoes in a spicy tomato sauce
pimientos	peppers
pimientos de padrón	small peppers, with the odd hot one thrown in
piña	pineapple
pisto	assortment of cooked vegetables, similar to ratatouille
plátano	banana
pollo	chicken
pulpo	octopus
queso	cheese
ración	a plateful of food
salchicha	sausage
setas	oyster mushrooms
sopa	soup
tapa	small serving of food
té	tea
tenedor	fork
tomate	tomato
tortilla (española)	potato omelette
tortilla francesa	plain omelette
vino (blanco/ rosado/tinto)	(white/rosé/red) wine
zumo	juice

Glossary

alcázar	Moorish fortified palace
avenida	avenue (usually abbreviated to avda)
ayuntamiento	town hall or council
barrio	suburb or neighbourhood
bodega	cellar or wine bar
calle	(usually abbreviated to C/) street or road
capilla mayor	chapel containing the high altar
cervecería	bar specializing in beers
correos	post office
corrida	bullfight
edificio	building
ermita	hermitage

estanco   small shop selling stamps and tobacco, recognizable by the brown and yellow signs bearing the word *tabacos*

iglesia   church

mercado   market

mirador   view point

Movida   Late 70s/early 80s creative explosion in Madrid, viewed as Spain's Swinging Sixties

Mudéjar   Spanish-Moorish architecture

museo   museum

parador   state-run hotel, usually housed in buildings of historic interest

plaza   square

plaza de toros   bullring

terraza   temporary summer outdoor bar

ROUGH GUIDES
TRAVEL SERIES

Travel guides to more than 250 destinations from Alaska to Zimbabwe

smooth travel

ROUGH GUIDES
REFERENCE SERIES

DON'T JUST TRAVEL!

small print & Index

SMALL PRINT

A Rough Guide to Rough Guides

Madrid DIRECTIONS is published by Rough Guides. The first *Rough Guide to Greece*, published in 1982, was a student scheme that became a publishing phenomenon. The immediate success of the book – with numerous reprints and a Thomas Cook Prize shortlisting – spawned a series that rapidly covered dozens of destinations. Rough Guides had a ready market among low-budget backpackers, but soon also acquired a much broader and older readership that relished Rough Guides' wit and inquisitiveness as much as their enthusiastic, critical approach. Everyone wants value for money, but not at any price. Rough Guides soon began supplementing the "rougher" information about hostels and low-budget listings with the kind of detail on restaurants and quality hotels that independent-minded visitors on any budget might expect, whether on business in New York or trekking in Thailand. These days the guides offer recommendations from shoestring to luxury and cover a large number of destinations around the globe, including almost every country in the Americas and Europe, more than half of Africa, and most of Asia and Australasia. Rough Guides now publish:

- Travel guides to more than 200 worldwide destinations
- Dictionary phrasebooks to 22 major languages
- Maps printed on rip-proof and waterproof Polyart™ paper
- Music guides running the gamut from Opera to Elvis
- Reference books on topics as diverse as the Weather and Shakespeare
- World Music CDs in association with World Music Network

Visit **www.roughguides.com** to see our latest publications.

Publishing information

This 1st edition published January 2004 by **Rough Guides Ltd**, 80 Strand, London WC2R 0RL
345 Hudson St, 4th Floor, New York, NY 10014, USA

Distributed by the Penguin Group
Penguin Books Ltd, 80 Strand, London WC2R 0RL
Penguin Group (USA), 375 Hudson Street, NY 10014, USA
Penguin Group (Australia), 487 Maroondah Highway, PO Box 257, Ringwood, Victoria 3134, Australia
Penguin Group (Canada), 10 Alcorn Avenue, Toronto, ON M4V 1E4, Canada
Penguin Group (NZ), 182–190 Wairau Road, Auckland 10, New Zealand
Typeset in Bembo and Helvetica to an original design by Henry Iles.
Printed in China.

192pp includes index.
A catalogue record for this book is available from the British Library.

ISBN 1-84353-410-X

The publishers and authors have done their best to ensure the accuracy and currency of all the information in **Madrid DIRECTIONS**; however, they can accept no responsibility for any loss, injury, or inconvenience sustained by any traveller as a result of information or advice contained in the guide.

1   3   5   7   9   8   6   4   2

Help us update

We've gone to a lot of effort to ensure that the first edition of **Madrid DIRECTIONS** is accurate and up-to-date. However, things change – places get "discovered", opening hours are notoriously fickle, restaurants and rooms raise prices or lower standards. If you feel we've got it wrong or left something out, we'd like to know, and if you can remember the address, the price, the phone number, so much the better.

We'll credit all contributions, and send a copy of the next edition (or any other DIRECTIONS guide or Rough Guide if you prefer) for the best letters. Everyone who writes to us and isn't already a subscriber will receive a copy of our full-colour thrice-yearly newsletter. Please mark letters: **"Madrid DIRECTIONS Update"** and send to: Rough Guides, 80 Strand, London WC2R 0RL, or Rough Guides, 4th Floor, 345 Hudson St, New York, NY 10014. Or send an email to **mail@roughguides.com**.

Have your questions answered and tell others about your trip at **www.roughguides.atinfopop.com**.

Rough Guide credits

Text editor: Clifton Wilkinson
Layout: Dan May
Photography: Ian Aitken
Cartography: Ed Wright
Picture editor: Jj Luck

Proofreader: Diane Margolis
Production: Julia Bovis
Design: Henry Iles
Cover art direction: Chloe Roberts

The author

Simon Baskett is a freelance writer and journalist who lives and works in Madrid with his wife, Trini, and children, Patrick and Laura. He's a long-suffering Atlético Madrid fan, and has not given up hope they might do "the double" again. His ambition is to win El Gordo (the huge Christmas lottery) and retire to a local bar. Simon is also author of the **Rough Guide to Madrid** and a co-author of the **Rough Guide to Spain**.

Acknowledgements

Special thanks to Trini once again for all her hard work and patience, and to Patrick and Laura for just being themselves. Thanks, too, go to Lucy, Dave, Dominic and Clifton, and all those who gave recommendations or advice for this book. Additional thanks to Ian for the photos, Jj for the picture editing, Chloe for the cover and Ed for the maps.

Photo credits

All images © Rough Guides except the following:

Front cover picture: Cervantes Monument © Jose Fuste, Corbis
Back cover picture: Palacio Real © Getty
p.4 Tilework of the Madrid bear and strawberry tree, in the Plaza Juan Pujol © P. Robinson/Robert Harding
p.5 Reina Sofía Museum © Sylvian Grandadam/Robert Harding
p.9 Casa Patas poster © DK Images
p.10 The Prado © Peter Wilson/Axiom
p.10 The Coal Barges by Vincent van Gogh © Francis G. Mayer/Corbis
p.11 Reina Sofía © Kim Sayer/DK Images
p.11 Palacio Real © Kim Sayer/DK Images
p.13 Madrid Zoo © Despotovic Dusko/Corbis Sygma
p.14 El Chicote © Peter Wilson/DK Images
p.15 Drag Queen © Carlos Guevara/Reuters/Corbis
p.20 Portrait of Henry VIII by Hans Holbein the Younger © Francis G. Mayer/Corbis
p.20 Las Meninas by Diego Rodriguez de Silva y Velázquez
p.21 Guernica by Pablo Picasso
p.21 Two Old Men Eating by Francisco Jose de Goya y Lucientes
p.21 The Garden of Earthly Delights by Hieronymus Bosch
p.23 Atocha Station © Kim Sayer/DK Images
p.24 Fiesta de San Isidro © Anders Ryman/Alamy
p.24 Philip II by Sir Anthonis Moro
p.25 Self Portrait, 1815 by Francisco Jose de Goya y Lucientes
p.25 Francisco Franco © Bettmann/Corbis
p.25 Pedro Almodóvar © Reuters/Corbis
p.26 Swimming pool © Sonia Gómez/Hotel Emperador
p.27 Chestnut seller © Ioannis Semitsoglou/Alamy
p.27 Christmas lights in Plaza Mayor © Marco Cristofori/Corbis
p.29 Botín © Peter Wilson/DK Images
p.30 Glass of sherry © Royalty-Free/Corbis
p.30 Viva Madrid © Peter Wilson/DK Images

p.31 Bar © Naki Kouyioumtzis/Axiom
p.32 Tapas © Peter Wilson/Axiom
p.34 Bullfighting © Steve J. Benbow/Axiom
p.35 Atlético Madrid fans parade their flag © Reuters/Corbis
p.35 Casa Patas poster © DK Images
p.37 Museo Lazaro Galdiano © Kim Sayer/DK Images
p.37 Real Fábrica de Tapices © The Royal Tapestry Factory
p.39 El Pardo © Max Alexander/DK Images
p.40 Festival of San Isidro © Ray Roberts/Alamy
p.41 Christmas in city centre © Steve Hamblin/Alamy
p.41 Semana Santa Fiesta © David Noton/Alamy
p.41 El Entierro de la Sardina © Zigzag Images/Alamy
p.41 Dos de Mayo © Franz-Marc Frei/Corbis
p.43 Gay Pride Parade © Andrea Comas/Reuters/Corbis
Full page: City Centre at night, Madrid © N. Francis/Robert Harding
p.93 *The Witches' Sabbath* or *The Great He-Goat*, c.1821-23 (oil on canvas) by Francisco Jose de Goya y Lucientes (1746-1828), Prado, Madrid, Spain/www.bridgeman.co.uk
p.95 *Dream Caused by the Flight of a Bee around a Pomegranate One Second before Waking*, 1944 (oil on canvas) by Salvador Dali (1904-89) Thyssen-Bornemisza Collection, Madrid, Spain/www.bridgeman.co.uk
p.103 Train at Atocha © Kim Sayer/DK Images
p.103 Real Fábrica de Tapices © The Royal Tapestry Factory
p.116 Pacha disco © Davide Bozzetti
p.119 Dama de Elche © Archivo Iconografico, S.A./Corbis
p.125 Zalacaín © George Wright/Axiom
p.147 El Greco painting of Toledo © Francis G. Mayer/Corbis

Index

Map entries are in colour

INDEX